OpenHR

The human capital framework
for a blended workforce

Jeremy Blain

Dr. Rochelle Haynes

Praise for *OpenHR*

"Open HR is a groundbreaking guide that provides the essential framework for embracing the blended workforce, a necessity in today's rapidly evolving work environment. Jeremy Blain and Dr Rochelle Haynes brilliantly articulate how organizations can harness the power of both permanent and independent talent to drive innovation, collaboration, and success. This book is a must-read for any leader looking to stay ahead in the war for talent by creating a truly inclusive and high-performing workforce."

– **John Winsor**, Founder and Chairman – Open Assembly; Executive in Residence – Laboratory for Innovation Sciences at Harvard; Co-Author of 'Open Talent - Leveraging the Global Workforce to Solve Your Biggest Challenges'

"Rigid and hierarchical structures are being replaced by more fluid, self-managed teams in the digital age. This requires a new way of thinking about people, their relationship with work, with organisations and with each other. Letting go of outdated conventions will unlock prosperity in the future of work, as Rochelle and Jeremy articulate brilliantly in this book."

– **Alex Hirst and Lizzie Penny**, Co-Authors of No.1 Sunday Times Bestseller 'Workstyle; A Revolution for Wellbeing, Productivity and Society'

Welcome to the Blended Workforce Revolution

"The blended workforce revolution will make the hyper-customisation of employee engagement a reality. For this, mindsets, behaviours, processes, and systems, including technology and law, will need to evolve globally in organisations. Independent workers have similar intrinsic and extrinsic needs and rights as any employee. Then, we can build a motivated, innovative, and high-performing blended workforce together, working side by side, hand in hand, as one powerful team."

– **Kaumudi Goda**, People, Leadership & Culture Strategist | Lawyer | ICF Certified Coach | Speaker | Board Director | C-Suite Advisor | Best Selling Author

"That idea that we shouldn't treat someone working independently in a similar way to someone on a permanent contract is a dangerous thing that will ultimately lead to bad behaviour and lack of success. We abuse remote workers at our peril."

– **Nicholas Mellors**, Director of Innovation Nottinghamshire

"I wanted to get out of the world. I felt stuck working a nine-to-five job, spending 2 to 3 hours commuting, so by the time I got home from work, I had no energy left. I knew that if I was able to work remotely, I could travel. As soon as I did that, it just freed up so much more inspiration in my life for me to give more to my work."

– **Sarah Azim**, Graphic Designer, Thailand

"I like that my clients understand we are human, that we are doing work for them, and that we are not robots."

– **Monique Welch**, CEO, The Press Fixer, Toronto

Dedications from the Authors

I would like to dedicate this book to the global human resources and human capital experts who are navigating the new world of work and the transformative workforce. It's good to know that our leaders, managers, and people at all levels, whether permanent or independent employees, are in good hands.

I would also like to dedicate this book to hard working gig workers, independent contractors, and digital nomads around the world, pioneering new ways to work and delivering value for customers everywhere.

You are a huge part of how work is evolving for the future, and the future is now. Thank you.

– Jeremy Blain

I am dedicating this book to the entrepreneurs, leaders, managers, and HR professionals who love what they do and have been demanding an evolution of work and traditional mindsets towards work. We see you and hear you and will continue to dedicate our professional lives to being the drivers of this change.

I also dedicate this to workers, especially our younger generations of workers, who have made their shifting expectations known, dared to challenge the status quo, and are fighting for a better work-life experience. This one's for you!

– Dr. Rochelle Haynes

Glossary of Key Terms

Please refer to the back of this book: 'OpenHR Glossary of Glossaries - The definitive list of terms for the OpenHR world'.

Open Talent

- A globally dispersed pool of highly skilled talent that can be accessed remotely by companies via online platforms and can work from anywhere.

Blended workforce

- A dynamic mixture of internal full-time or part-time employees, and independent talent offering services for short-term projects or longer-term contracts.

Digital Nomads

Location-independent talent who has little to no physical interaction with their employer/employers. Also called telecommuter or teleworkers, these individuals may fall into two main categories:

1. **Independent contractors** - Those contracted to work with an organisation for a specific project or period.

2. **Traditional job holders** - Those who hold full-time jobs but pursue a non-traditional work style.

Key traits: Well-educated, highly skilled, and digitally savvy

Gig Workers:

- Independent contractors are hired mainly via online gig platforms, which act as intermediaries between the customer and the employing company. These contractors will be hired online to complete crowdsourcing or on-demand work, which may determine the level of physical contact with a company's customers.

WHY YOU AND YOUR BUSINESS NEED TO ADOPT AN OPENHR FRAMEWORK

The world of work continues to change at a head-spinning pace, and most companies are not prepared to manage this change effectively. Technological developments, shifting work expectations, and global pandemic in the early 2020s have been the biggest accelerators of digital transformation since the iPhone launch in 2007. What was once a gradual and measured increase in remote and independent working, has now formalised into an explosion of new and modified working practices.

While remote work was already the norm for a growing minority, a significant majority of employed, in-house workers now desire roles with greater flexibility, including independent work and contracting. As we emerged from the COVID-19 pandemic, this accelerating trend was called the 'Great Resignation' and became a very real trend.

In the UK, for example, this was reflected by vacancies exceeding the number of unemployed people in the permanent labour market[1]. This trend reaches across generations from millennials and Generation Z intakes to a large proportion of Generation X'ers, the so-called

---

1   https://www.securitywatchdog.org.uk/latest-news/uk-job-vacancies-higher-than-number-of-unemployed-for-first-time-in-50-years/

'leaders in waiting' who are supposed to lead our organisations into the next decade and beyond. This represents a worrying talent and experience drain for many organisations, leading to a power shift in recruitment and employment terms.

This trend has evolved into the Great Regret, The Great Rethink and, for a small proportion, the Great Rehire. More recently, history looks set to repeat itself with The Great Reshuffle. It is hard to keep up.

We argue the focus should be on getting back to plain great! No matter what the employment designation, job role, permanent, part-time, or independent worker.

A more worrying development on the US front that has further increased the freelancer trend is ongoing mass layoffs in large tech firms (e.g. Meta, X, Amazon, Stripe). Between November 2022 and January 2023, almost 200,000 employees globally have been let go due to organisational cutbacks, further undermining the notion of job security. In addition, while the evolution of generative AI, Blockchain, and hyper-automation is potentially creating new jobs, it is almost certainly adding to further layoffs as we head through the next few years of more rapid and broader automation.

Let's turn to the employees who have more power to choose. Employers must work much harder to attract, engage and retain talent. Traditionally, this was the other way around. According to Microsoft and LinkedIn surveys in 2024 almost half of all employees internationally were thinking of quitting their jobs over the following year.[2] This is staggering. Accenture points to a broader competitive landscape being navigated by recruiters and employers, considering they are not just competing for talent in a specific role or level but as a

---

2   https://www.linkedin.com/business/talent/blog/talent-acquisition/time-to-prepare-for-great-reshuffle

share of an individual's available time, life choices, and more flexible work preferences. This calls for greater competitive agility for many.[3]

This is 'War for Talent 4.0,' with companies struggling to find the right people, at the right time and with the right expertise.

As Josh Bersin observed, HR leaders have the opportunity to lead the business community for the first time in history.[4] Significant societal events, including war, the pandemic, climate change, technological developments, The Great Resignation, The Great Regret, Loud Layoffs in the tech industry and more, are happening now, so where are all these people going, and what are they doing? They are heading largely to what we call the Open Talent Economy: Many are consulting, working, and contracting with the very same organisations they left, while others are broadening their scope and working on multiple projects or tasks with multiple clients[5]. This is done flexibly, with distributed working being the primary modus operandi.

THE NEW WORK REVOLUTION

These trends accelerate the movement into independent and new kinds of work and force organisations everywhere to rethink the true nature of their future workforce and how it is made up. For too long, employers have adopted a paternalistic approach within the organisation, a dynamic which often translated to workers having less organisational control and being deployed as deemed appropriate. While this mindset has been advanced since the industrial revolution and treated as the default way to manage and organise work, external

---

3   https://www.accenture.com/gb-en/insights/competitive-agility-index

4   https://joshbersin.com/2023/01/
      predictions-for-2023-redefining-work-the-workforce-and-hr/

5   https://www.mbopartners.com/state-of-independence/

shocks and changing expectations have demanded a review of existing work arrangements. Therefore, it is clear that we need a new human capital framework that values all workers, regardless of their employment designation or preference. One that celebrates the broader, more diverse talent inside and outside of our organisations, which excels, grows, innovates, and collaborates in ways that will fuel the dynamic nature of our businesses everywhere, regardless of size, industry, or specialism. The time is right to tap into a more open human capital economy and embrace the revolution happening under our noses: The decentralisation of work!

So, what do we mean by terms like 'Open talent' and 'Open Economy'? Surely, by nature, the labour market is open, with digitalisation enabling and accelerating work across borders. Using the word 'open' in this context we refer to a shift in thinking to an open view and open mindset about the talent we use in our organisations. On the flipside, a growing talent pool that is open to embracing different working practices, preferences and opportunities.

As we emerged from the COVID-19 pandemic in the early 2020s, there was evidence of a significant rise in flexible or 'gig' workers, including digital nomads: those who are location-independent and work primarily from their laptops or mobile devices. In fact, by the end of 2023, one in ten workers, globally, were gig workers[6]. It has changed the entire legacy approach to attraction, recruitment, growth, and retention of employees, which once focused solely on permanent workers (and additional 'managed services').

---

6   https://www.worldbank.org/en/news/press-release/2023/09/07/demand-for-online-gig-work-rapidly-rising-in-developing-countries

DEFINING THE NEW HUMAN CAPITAL TALENT POOL

Open economy / Open workforce - The full ecosphere of non-permanently employed workers globally. This is often defined as the mix of the gig workforce and the more formalised group of independent consultants, freelancers, interim workers, short-term employed expertise resources, and general or specific independent workers often offering longer-term services in the corporate space. For example, in supporting small, medium, large, and multinational organisations as a more formalised part of the blended workforce - the mix of permanent, permanent part-time and open workforce.

Gig economy / Gig workforce - A subset of the Open economy where independent workers offer a specific service for a specified price, often as one-off transactions or projects. For example, there has been a noted increase in the number of translators, interpreters, copywriters, and proofreaders across the open economy. In organisational terms, many small and medium organisations may now favour working with 'gigsters' for services like tech support, marketing design, branding, and social media promotions. It is more specialised yet cheaper than a traditional marketing and communications agency. And the service or product can be just as good, if not better.

Now, in an age where talent can choose when, where and how they work, there is a new need to focus on a fully blended workforce consisting of both permanent and independent workers. Yet, despite the catalytic effects of the pandemic in the early 2020s, which lifted the lid on the wellbeing agenda and how people want to work, few organisations employ a structured approach to managing their remote and independent stakeholders, closely aligned to their permanent workforce. Few organisations have considered the need to integrate a fully blended workforce. Not many have yet adopted a human resources management model and framework more suited to the trends we have highlighted. We can no longer ignore and the associated needs of this evolved workforce, in line with the transformational times we are living and working through and the changing needs of employees or prospective employees, whatever their designation.

THE OPENHR MANIFESTO

There is an opportunity here for organisations to work better with blended talent in a way that suits all parties, with more of a level playing field for both permanent and contingent workers. However, this will not be achieved through an exclusive focus on attracting a shrinking pool of permanent employees. Considering the newly created opportunities offered by embracing a blended workforce and the rich talent pool of permanent and independent workers or long-term contractors is essential.

> **In other words, the Open Economy demands a response from organisations to reflect this with a transformed, more open, HR framework. Underpinned by a new way of marshalling human capital and an evolved way of engaging with permanent employees and Open talent, the new, formalised workforce of today and tomorrow.**

In our February 2020 white paper on the blended workforce revolution, we predicted the above changes and urged organisations to ditch the traditional mindset and approaches to human resources management. The rise of the gig economy has expanded over the years to include less skilled work and highly skilled jobs. While this means that companies now have a wider, globally dispersed pool of key talent available, poor management and lack of cultural fit result in short-term value delivery and little long-term value creation.

As we revisited the research in 2024, it has become obvious that most organisations still fail to appreciate the diversity and dynamic shifts in the shifting workforce. As a result, they are not adequately engaging or benefitting from an increasingly agile and growing talent pool. This talent pool has too often been thrown into a generic mix of 'managed services' rather than being considered a formalised workforce in its own right, despite the seismic workforce shifts of the recent past. As part of a managed services mix, this potentially high-value ad hoc workforce has not traditionally been given appropriate organisational support and management, which could have helped build rapid mutual value, longer-term relations where desired, and more.

Our ongoing research reinforces the call for a bold new human resources manifesto and framework as we eye the near future. Up to now, there does not appear to have been a consistent approach for organisations to access. As a result, we have created the OpenHR framework. This framework recognises the blended workforce and hybrid/distributed work trends and the need for a new approach to human resources management, regardless of employee designation, location, or preferred ways of working. This is not so much about managing permanent employees anymore but managing a more collaborative, mixed work: a blended group of permanent and independent talent who are empowered, highly collaborative and asynchronous in their working practices. This would be reflected by a repurposed leadership and line management structure that supports 'Work-Collective' collaboration, growth and delivery of specific tasks or longer-term objectives.

We supplement our ongoing research by extracting data from an increased number of sources, including thousands of social media platform inputs. This allowed us to understand trends and sentiments concerning the blended workforce, gig work, hybrid, and distributed work. Our research explored employee and employer perspectives, going deeper into emotional connections, feelings, and hard business trends.

This research was completed with 'MySocialPulse' and represents the latest Artificial Intelligence (AI) research thinking, methodology and real-time insights. Our updated data set in 2023 comprised over 20,000 profiles across multiple industry sectors, consisting of organisational leaders and management, permanent employees, independent contractors, and gig workers, representing multiple levels of experience across over 62 countries spanning four continents. We highlight the data outputs in Chapter 1: 'The Pain Points.'

In writing this book, we aim to build the rationale for fundamental people management transformation through market analysis, our own research, and the latest industry white papers that have been circulated on the topic.

This strong rationale-building will shift mindsets and create readiness for action. Therefore, the rest of the book deals with the 'how-to' around implementing OpenHR. This comes with comprehensive new models, interviews, advice, and examples from industry experts leading the way, toolkits, and ready-to-use templates to prepare any organisation to embark on a step-by-step execution journey.

Securing implementation success and building momentum will help you embed the change in your organisation.

This book is what your company needs to navigate the new work landscape successfully. Read on to discover how OpenHR can be your organisation's reality and new human resources standard.

Chapter 1

THE PAIN POINTS AND OPPORTUNITIES

Work priorities are shifting. The move towards independent and freelance work is growing, and company demands for globally dispersed expertise are higher than ever.

While the gig economy has been around for more than 10 years, its uptake has increased as individuals demand greater flexibility, autonomy, and mobility in their work lives. One Indian job site, Teamlease, reported more than 11,000 placements for gig workers, representing a 2.5-fold increase in demand and a more positive perception of the value the independent workforce can bring.[7]

Another survey by MBO Partners reported a 49% increase in digital nomads in 2020 compared with 2019 and a 131% increase between 2019 and 2023.[8] Despite this increase, most companies are still not ready to accommodate 'open talent,' with most firms offering little in the way of decent pay, benefits, training, suitable working arrangements, recognition, or long-term opportunities. In many cases, the reason is that the company environment and HR policies are not designed to accommodate these independent stakeholders.

---

7 https://group.teamlease.com/tlmedias/78-of-employers-are-optimistic-about-gig-workers-teamlease-edtech-report-highlights-key-skills-for-long-term-success/

8 https://www.mbopartners.com/state-of-independence/

To truly embrace and take advantage of the changing workforce, companies need to approach the engagement and management of freelancers/open talent in a more purposeful and structured way. Recognising this need, we have used our research findings to create the OpenHR model. This is an actionable framework developed to help human resources and organisational development managers create an environment that is truly inclusive of all types of workers and can benefit from changing work dynamics.

OUR RESEARCH THROUGH THE 2020S

We uncovered key trends in our 2020 research. We predicted that by 2027, many businesses' workforces would comprise approximately 50% permanent workers and 50% independents (on contracts ranging from short-term to long-term). Four years later, this is accelerating due to the pandemic of the early 2020s and the ongoing acceleration of whole business transformation on many corporate and public sector agendas.

To update our 2020 findings, we conducted brand new research in 2023 and early 2024 to understand how the accelerating 'gig work' or, more recently, the broader 'Open talent marketplace' and independent contracting trends were shifting how organisations were hiring, structuring and more. Beyond managed services and into a formalised structured modern workforce, blending permanent workers with independent workers, supported by new human capital management and organisational structures.

On top of our committed research, we also interviewed business leaders, respected global HR professionals, organisational design specialists and human capital management experts. These interviews are spread throughout the book. Some are in full, some as quotes, and some as specific comments on selected points we have raised.

We took emerging, innovative routes to complete our research, supplemented with more traditional pulse surveys and interviews. That said, the main methods and techniques applied to generate our new research outputs do not follow the traditional methods.

What has been used is a proprietary Generative Artificial Intelligence (AI) and a Natural Language Processing (NLP) engine, which is called My Social Pulse (MSP), pioneered by Divya Prasanth and Janine Miles, co-founders of MySocialPulse and BlockRank Ltd.

This approach secures real-time views and opinions expressed by real people on platforms such as Quora, Reddit, Glassdoor, X, formerly known as Twitter, and more to understand the emotional sentiments at play as much as the decisions and actions people make as permanent workers or open talent.

This brand-new research methodology has allowed us to instantly tap into numerous data sources, including social media platforms and any site that provides reviews. The powerful AI engine is applied to thousands of data sources, moving insight into foresight.

RESEARCH BREAKDOWN (GLOBAL DISTRIBUTION)

Quora - 4,467 surveyed inputs

Reddit - 5,204 surveyed inputs

Glassdoor - 3,455 surveyed inputs

X, formally known as Twitter - 7,034 tweets analysed.

A total of **20,160** survey points

Making this up is a mix of permanent employees (21%), part-time employed workers (11%), open talent: gig workers, independent contractors, and freelancers (42%), higher education and unemployed adults (18%), and others (8%).

TOPICS WE ANALYSED AND BROKE DOWN THROUGHOUT OUR RESEARCH:

- Working from home

- The open talent economy (Gig workers, independent contractors, freelancers…)

- The blended workforce

- Diversity, equity, and inclusion matters

- Hybrid Working

- Culture in the workplace

- Reward & recognition

The research focus has centred on the trends within the open talent economy (Giggers, independent workers, contractors, and free-lancers), the increased blending of the workforce (permanent workers and open talent working side by side as one valued workforce), and the sentiments, both positive and negative, according to workers themselves, whatever their designation.

The research was structured in a way that helped us quickly and easily get to the most important sentiments being discussed across multiple social media platforms. We did this by breaking the research outputs into three distinct areas:

- Pros & Cons of permanent versus independent working

- Potential Questions raised through the research feedback

- Summary Points of note, including multiple SWOT Analyses & Behavioural (Sentiment) Visuals to make the data come alive

While we summarise some key research points in this book, our wider data is used more concretely in our workshops and consulting as deep dives into the facts, sentiments and resulting actions or impacts.

Our research reflects the speed of change in our industries and across businesses, enabling annual updates and ongoing pulse sentiment analysis for immediate data while always incorporating new research inputs and evolving case studies and real-world examples.

For example, we secured input from various companies practising a movement to a more open talent-centred workforce for this book: A mix of permanent, permanent part-time, and independent workers as the valued employee ecosphere. We asked them for their return on experience and for quantitative evidence where it has been successful. You can find a summary of each later on in this chapter:

- A major multinational cloud-native software innovator headquartered in Europe.

- A global software, distributed cloud, and data science startup headquartered in North America

- A global manufacturing company servicing the automotive industry since 1919, headquartered in Japan.

THE CONTEXT FOR OUR RESEARCH

(adapted from MySocialPulse research report: MySocialPulse for Jeremy Blain and Dr. Rochelle Haynes)

The workspace is an integral part of most of our lives. The type of environment and culture that we interact with has the potential to impact our physical and mental health greatly. Employees, whether employed or contingent workers, are becoming more aware of certain unavoidable aspects of their jobs, plus the positive and negative impacts that this brings to work-life balance, job security, feelings of inclusion, exclusion, reward, recognition, and empowerment. All of which can promote but also impact personal growth and engagement. It has become imperative for the corporate world to pay attention to such issues and address them accordingly in the best interest of mutual benefit.

The major topic of discussion in today's rapidly evolving workspace scenario is the "privilege" to choose how to work, from where to work and who to work with and complemented by formalising hybrid and distributed working models. This is linked to a major theme running through our research on the impact of the increasingly blended workforce (permanent/independent) and that of the open talent economy, as a formalised part of modern business, on the workplace and its people.

Open talent within the global economy constantly searches for better rights and privileges for themselves. For corporations, human capital is an organisation's greatest asset, balancing the company's operations, growth, transformation plans and implementing their strategic vision can bring its own set of challenges. Meeting their permanent and open talent needs while competing with other businesses for the talent and skill sets required is a delicate balance of managing costs, restructuring legacy business models and, in some cases, reinventing altogether the human capital management framework to make it more fit for purpose when reflecting the modern workforce and workplaces. This is at the heart of our sentiment-based research outputs.

One notable piece of sentiment data concerns work location preferences, as well as their level of flexible and balanced choice or at least where they have a flexible and balanced choice. Most of those surveyed (both permanent, open talent and those not yet in employment) overwhelmingly prefer hybrid working or pure distributed working (including working from home or any location permanently). The preference and positive sentiment towards this are so marked that there is evidence that a large percentage of permanent employees and hired open talent would actively look to secure another role, company or gig if they were required to be in the office full-time. This is where a rethink is urgently required in many small, medium, large, and multinational organisations. We need a reimagining of how human capital across all its lenses is managed, where people should be located, how the workforce can be more efficiently and effectively managed, targeted and rewarded, and how organisations should redesign themselves to be more modern and attractive to all forms of talent - whether permanent or open.

HOW WE CONDUCTED OUR RESEARCH

Our method of research, this time around, heavily leans on social media. Quite deliberately. This is real-time feedback, and sentiment data corporate enterprise should be far more attuned to than is reality. It enables immediate feedback, foresight, decision-making power, and is a gateway to more rapid action. It also represents the social pulse of the wider workforce, be they permanent or independent workers, at every level.

Social media platforms like X, Reddit, Quora, Glassdoor, and others have been pivotal in extracting information on how people generally would like things to go. They also offer great lessons to corporate leaders on how they can implement positive changes, at lightning speed, within their companies to be more attractive to prospective employees and their existing employees and how they better retain Talent for the future.

This speed is driven by the immediacy of the social media data we can now access, analysed in real-time through MySocialPulse's proprietary Generative AI, leading to real-time response and feedback.

OUTPUTS FROM OUR RESEARCH

Results from our research indicated that embracing a more enlightened human capital framework was linked to having more skilled, informed HR professionals and senior leaders who understand the benefits of a truly flexible, borderless, and diverse workforce.

According to the positive sentiment analysis we conducted with permanent and independent workers, the main 'human' benefits are:

- Increased and improved collaboration

- A more autonomous, empowered workforce

- Greater performance support vs performance management.

- More open communication

- Formalised asynchronous working structures and processes

- Greater commitment to well-being, diversity, equity, and inclusion.

In fact, the blended, open workforce, by its very nature, moves the dial significantly in DE&I terms. This, in turn, makes for a happier organisation and a more positive culture for both permanent and independent workers.

- A broader diversity of thinking, moving away from recruitment moulds of the past and embracing new, different thinking that could potentially open the door to innovation not yet considered.

- A new human capital framework creates a better deal for all employees, regardless of their designation (i.e. permanent or independent) and location.

But what about the impact on the numbers? The data suggests that businesses championing these areas will deliver better results than those that don't regard productivity and revenue. A double benefit is driving a clear bottom-line upside. The three 2023 and 2024 examples below support our research and have been used with kind permission from '*The Transformational Leadership Acceleration Institute*'[9]

1. **A major multinational cloud-native software innovator** that embraces the blended workforce as the most suited structure for their business demonstrated the following hard numbers when analysing results over 2023 and 2024:

   ◦ Productivity double-digit benefit

   ◦ Attraction of talent - moved from a strategy of 'push' first to 'pull' - The word was out, and they were attracting an increased number of permanent and independent workers, who were being pulled into their orbit based on positive sentiment data across channels and formal business networks

---

9   www.tlai.org

- Turnover of existing talent dropped from 44% turnover (as a global average) to under 25% as employees felt more fulfilled and valued. This included greater loyalty from independent workers who went from beyond project focus to company focus, feeling more like a part of a valued team.

2. **A global software, distributed cloud and data science startup** providing data management and analytics services to multiple vertical industry sectors has enjoyed rapid expansion across borders through an open talent policy as the cultural foundation for its business and the people in it. They attracted permanent workers and experienced (GenX) independent experts with experience in strategic expansion, digital transformation and more. They could use talent in several different ways, depending on their needs. They point to this flexible use of talent as 'doing away with' traditional job descriptions and job role pigeonholing. Instead, they encourage strategic and operational contributions based on specific expertise and experience.

   This has become a 'fluid open talent' policy in their business for permanent workers as much as independent talent. Based on our collaborations with this client, we have secured the data to prove return on investment and experience (ROI and ROE) over 2023:

   - Employee satisfaction Net Promoter Score (NPS) of 9.2 (up from 8.7 the previous year)

   - Customer satisfaction measures also drive an improved NPS of 8.8 from 7.9 > rapid progress, and they will create more customer advocates in the next year.

- Company performance revenue increase over the past 2 years shows double-digit growth, despite a pandemic growth spike they were comparing against

- EBIT up by 2.3 percentage points over the same period

3. **A global manufacturing company since 1919,** supplying the automotive and aerospace industries, has revolutionised its white-collar and blue-collar workforce, rewards, and benefits through embracing a blended workforce using both permanent workers, permanent part-time workers, and a workforce from the open economy - Most notably across parts design, workflow automation and a 24/7 plant-based workforce. Making independent workers a formal part of their employee base in many parts of the world while saving on both white-collar infrastructure and recruitment and blue-collar costs (especially associated with unionised permanent workforces).

In addition, since 2022, at the strategic transformation level, independent experts and workers have been employed on 6-month contracts to support a huge data science overhaul and the implementation of an associated platforms ecosystem, people engagement plan and new, streamlined processes. This has broken down traditional silos and legacy leadership and management approaches, enabling a more horizontal structure and an unprecedented sponsorship of empowered working and decision-making at all levels, supported by coaching-led management supporters. It's been a cultural evolution as much as a business benefit.

The CFO explained that in the first quarter of 2023, productivity measures were "off the charts," with a 74% improvement at both manufacturing and corporate levels. He offered that breaking down traditional Japanese management structures and approaches and embracing a global open workforce have been the main drivers for success in both productivity terms and a first quarter 2023 double-digit growth that shows no signs of slowing.

The numbers above support mounting evidence for a more flexible, blended and talent-rich open workforce. It is no wonder that many more organisations globally (small, medium, and large) are considering or actively moving to an open talent model.

THE CONSEQUENCES OF NOT CONSIDERING AN OPEN WORKFORCE APPROACH:

Those who do not buy into an Open workforce model recognising current trends and adapting to them, risk employee drain. Fewer people will be attracted to the company for either a permanent job or a contract. Even more worrying is the risk of losing great talent already in the business. More worryingly, this talent drain is at all levels.

For example, following our sentiment research, there is a noted movement of Generation X'ers out of traditional permanent employee-based careers. GenX is the fastest growing population in the open economy, stating a preference to be out of the corporate world as permanent employees, preferring to re-enter as independent contractors. They are freer to choose, use their expertise in more targeted ways, and can be apart from corporate politics, challenges, and pressures. Particularly if they feel they are the 'leaders-in-waiting,' in organisations where there may still be a huge backlog of transformational issues, challenges, tasks, and opportunities that have yet to be moved forward coherently. Many are responding with a resounding 'no thanks' to that.

This is huge and should be a more worrying shift (than it appears) for many organisations. There are some who are simply not willing, or willing but not quick enough to change, as their so-called next C-Suite-in-waiting, our GenX'ers, seem to be turning their back on the challenge and voting with their feet. They don't want to take over the scope and scale of transformation and legacy issues that remain in some organisations. And who can blame them for leaving the laggers?

Embracing a more open and blended talent framework means organisations are ready and attentive to the growing talent pool, independent consultancy, and contracted expertise across the gig economy. They can then attract, excite, and engage experienced professionals and young, specialised talent when needed. They continue to build a mutual value-adding relationship without a formal permanent employee structure to fit it into.

THE WORKFORCE OF THE FUTURE, NOW

This research has also been pivotal in extracting information on how a range of talent worldwide would like things to go. Our outputs offer a great lesson to corporate and human capital leaders on how they can implement positive changes within their companies.

The idea that drives today's workforce is not just about getting a great role, paid, promoted, etc. **It's about fulfilment - or meaningful work and collaborations.**

An open human capital management framework with an open talent approach offers flexibility, suitability, fulfilment, and greater two-way value when considering the employee (whether permanent or open talent) and the organisation itself.

Perhaps the biggest shift we see as of 2024 is the formalisation of Open talent as a central part of the global workforce, supported by a parallel overhaul of working contracts, conditions, and rewards (beyond contract paying) and a fundamental shift away from 'managed services' to a truly valued part of any organisation's human capital.

It is no surprise that the open economy in the United States alone, by the end of 2023, was made up of over 75 million independents (predicted to rise to over 90 million by 2028), contributing more than 1.5 trillion USD to the US GDP.[10]

For many corporations, there is, as a result, a more urgent need to define human resources and human capital management structures to recognise a formalised blended workforce. Not as a temporary measure but as the way things are and will continue to be. There is a clear benefit of doing so, according to businesses and their leaders, when we consider the four powerful stats below curated by Symmetrical.[11]

1. 33% of organisations say they're using alternative arrangements for IT, 25% for operations, 15% for R&D and 15% for marketing (Deloitte).

2. According to 62% of executives, an external workforce enables them to improve the company's overall financial performance (SAP Fieldglass). For instance, companies economise on employee benefits and office overheads.

---

10   https://www.statista.com/statistics/921593/
     gig-economy-number-of-freelancers-us/

11   https://www.symmetrical.ai/blog/
     jak-bedzie-wygladal-rynek-pracy-przyszlosci

3. Almost three-quarters of executives cite the importance of the open workforce in sourcing hard-to-find skills (SAP Fieldglass).

4. 3 in 5 leaders increasingly prefer to "rent," "borrow," or "share" talent with other companies, making their full-time staff smaller (Harvard Business School).

When we put a more strategic hat on, this makes sense. The blended workforce, combining permanent and open talent, enables the sourcing of expertise from anywhere for any role. It is, by definition, a more diverse, equitable and inclusive system; it reinforces the importance and normalising of hybrid or distributed working, rather than being one hundred per cent office-based; it provides human capital resources economies and can be more flexibly scaled up or scaled down as required. It also allows any company to employ experts or specialists they simply may not be able to afford on a permanent contract, which is made possible by the open economy.

This is nothing less than an enterprise-wide human capital movement. A movement driving an evolution of business models and HR structures. It impacts how business will continue to evolve, how business is and will be done, and how the fabric of business needs to shift in line with the workforce of tomorrow; today.

This human capital movement has led to a more concrete focus on the foundation stones, to start an OpenHR approach in the right way, protecting both permanent and independent employee rights.

This was highlighted in our own 'Rise of the Blended Workforce'[12] research. We found six key areas of focus for successful engagement and implementation of independent talent. A solid platform from which to formalise the blended workforce for your organisation,

---

12   https://performanceworks.global/the-gig-hr-experts/

now. Going beyond managed services and into 'how we do things around here'.

1. Clearer and more realistic objectives from the start

2. More on-the-job support up front for both permanent and non-permanent workers

3. Flexibility around working style for all employees.

4. Reduce complexity when working, collaborating, and communicating together.

5. Fair contracts and respectful payment terms (particularly for open talent being employed on short or longer-term contracts or projects)

6. Executive leaders and line management who are ready for the shift and moving their focus from supervision to coaching-led support. For all.

Unfortunately, many organisations still do not recognise their independent resources as valued members of the company or team they are working with, as explained here by one of our research interviewees.

"Putting people on precarious contracts
happens a lot in the gig economy and to
corporate contractor resources. That way,
they (clients) can offload risks onto you, saving
themselves money, taxes, health benefits,
etc. It's a very exploitative way of employing
people, and it puts a lot of risk on me."

– GRAPHIC DESIGNER AND DIGITAL
NOMAD, THAILAND, 2024

As there is indisputable proof that the blended workforce is now a reality and will only grow over the next few years, this should be a wake-up call for everyone. Corporate enterprises, businesses, and sectors are utilising independent workforces, and independent workers themselves must now think of how they formalise their contracts, negotiations, collaborations, and client focus. It's not all one way.

Prior to the next chapter, 'OpenHR,' we will reinforce some of these pain points, opportunities for HR professionals, and more, in discussion with a globally experienced human resources leader and practitioner, Linda Hughes.

We discuss the movement to an increasingly blended workforce, the implications for businesses globally and, especially, what needs to change in human capital management and HR expertise terms as organisations shift to a more open talent model, requiring a brand-new framework for how we manage our most valued asset. Our people. Whether they are permanent employees or independent talent on short-term or longer-term contracts.

THE CURRENT PAIN POINTS AND OPPORTUNITIES FROM A GLOBAL HR PRACTITIONER PERSPECTIVE

With Linda Hughes. HR Coach & Organisational Change Director; Dynamic Coach Ltd.

Jeremy Blain and Dr Rochelle Haynes: As we emerge into the new normal and welcome greater numbers of independent workers into our organisations, why do HR professionals need to rapidly rescale, upskill, and re-orientate themselves when considering a holistic blended workforce approach versus focusing on permanent employees and other 'managed services' when required?

Linda Hughes: This is a new phase of employment post the COVID-19 crisis, and in consideration of the distribution of people in work, according to ONS, "In October 2021, there were 34.8 million people in employed jobs with 75% being full-time employees and 4.3 million people self-employed, and just over 1 million job vacancies." While these are interesting figures, there is no actual breakdown of the distribution of job types advertised. Indeed, I think it would be quite difficult to get an overview of actual jobs and assignments in the marketplace, but needless to say, many workers are full-time in paid employment (PAYE) – and within those numbers are managed services. A further reference point David Blanchflower, a former member of the Bank of England's rate-setting monetary policy committee, referring to the number of people self-employed said: "The gig economy isn't necessarily bad, but it does show the changing nature of work – you also have to look at rising self-employment and short-term contracts in traditional jobs."

Jeremy Blain and Dr Rochelle Haynes: Quite naturally, the orientation of bringing somebody into the business has, therefore, been the permanent employee because of the longevity and relative investment into that person.

Linda Hughes: I totally agree with you; the route has a greater proportion of permanent workers, fixed-term contractors, and a very small number of temps, all as separate entities, with the last two being viewed as managed services. They are not seen as the 'workforce' holistically.

I also believe the word "workforce" represents a bit of an old-fashioned term and is linked with someone working for a single organisation, and clearly, this is not the case as we advance with people having a mix of jobs and contract terms. If we start to replace "employees or staff" with "workforce," it will have a much broader meaning, and that's the challenge of expanding the interpretation of the workforce.

Jeremy Blain and Dr Rochelle Haynes: Another interesting change until the turn of the century, we still had "careers for life," and now, though it may be 2-year hires. So, this point is massively important as a trigger point to transform and think about a new human capital framework in this respect when you also might have a contractor for the same time.

Linda Hughes: That's a really interesting point, and I agree with you that to recruit a Gen Z'er or millennial for 2 years is good going, and they would expect to get a new job after that period of time. However, it's not only millennials where we are finding job shifters; it's across the employment market. So, is there a different way to look at this challenge – I would say it's a bit like the phrase "cart before the horse." We have to switch our thinking around and instead of pulling together a job description that contains many elements – which in reality makes it attractive to the applicant – but in truth doesn't always end up being the job.

We take a different approach to scope a brief with expected outcomes and then resource against this need. It is a more agile approach, and it focuses on providing the worker with the opportunity to get the most out of the assignment instead of after two years evaluating why that person is leaving. It also drives the need for better career and talent management instead of job description writing and replaces the need to make the role permanent or a contract assignment.

Jeremy Blain and Dr Rochelle Haynes: This could really be a game changer, ultimately thinking about the resources required for a certain period or outcome and re-imaging certain job roles as solely perm and some as sole contractor, etc.

Linda Hughes: That is exactly right. It is clear to me that organisations need to review their people strategy and how they attract talent. A broader, multifaceted approach is required to manage the dimensions of resources that could be engaged equally. For example, adopting and building appropriate systems, allowing the organisation to capture a variety of resources as 'the workforce' (regardless of employment contract status) all in one place; this also needs to be aligned with country taxation reporting; otherwise, the argument is not to do it will be too simple and organisations will revert to permanent workers. Traditional systems don't have as many opportunities to capture that information in the way we need for now and the future. Current systems lock many HR professionals in traditional thinking or get bogged down by administrative tasks, equal pay job evaluations, diversity and inclusion measures and so on. They are important, but they take the focus away from evolving the current system and finding a new way to engage, support, and get the best out of our workforce.

Jeremy Blain and Dr Rochelle Haynes: If you reflect on the organisational needs, going back to the question here and specifically, "Why do HR professionals need to rescale, upskill and re-orientate themselves rapidly?" there are a bunch of strategic requirements, there are some operational tasks, and then there is something else – what's that for you?

Linda Hughes: For me, it's a mindset change that is required from the very top through to all levels and dimensions of our HR workforce, and this human-centred thinking must really come from the HR professional if we are to succeed and adapt how we work to match the modern workplace needs and the needs of human capital, regardless of their designation. Then, our first point of action is to think differently. It's our role to create business value through people – this shifts us from a cost centre to a value-added function. I think it will take time for our finance colleagues to agree with this, but we should be orienting ourselves to provide value instead of being seen as a support function.

Jeremy Blain and Dr Rochelle Haynes: Do you think they should be more commercial as well?

Linda Hughes: Yes, and I know that is not new – but it is keeping it fresh and appropriate for changing times. Being active on social media, being expert networkers, being researchers across multiple platforms to know the data and the resources that are available to benefit your hiring approach or engagement strategy and so on. Are all activities that should be regular events and not when someone is monitoring website traffic? A digital-first mindset is needed.

Jeremy Blain and Dr Rochelle Haynes: Let's talk a bit more about the future and the impact on job roles as you see it.

Linda Hughes: I think you might have gained the impression that I am a keen advocate of HR playing a lead role in helping the organisation think about the future of work, the changes in job roles, and what that means for the organisation. Obviously, each HR professional will approach this in their own way. But fundamentally, we shall get to a point where a high proportion of roles, as we know them today, will disappear, and we need to act now and plan for transition or retraining the workforce. Also, what new roles are required, where the skills are in the marketplace, how do we engage these people in our business, etc? This takes time, and time is limited, so as I have already mentioned, networking and external-facing HR professionals may well reach the resources they need more quickly. A further element is looking at the retraining of staff and how that could be fulfilled – creativity is a key skill that HR must start to show within their repertoire. Again, this is a shift back to the digital-first mindset and really understanding the different roles within the organisation because not every role and person can be retained going forward, and it is important to know how to enable them with appropriate technology and tools for the modern era.

So, your pitch is a lot stronger, as it proves you understand the business imperatives more deeply and can have more commercially oriented discussions with your stakeholders. That whole agenda and conversation should be led, measured, and followed up by HR as very specific ROI proofing, as much as return on the experience for all stakeholders. Something we have lost in some organisations.

Jeremy Blain and Dr Rochelle Haynes: That makes so much sense, Linda. What other specific knowledge, skills, and behaviours will benefit HR leaders, managers, and professionals as they lead the workforce framework transformation agenda for a digital world and the management of a blended workforce?

Linda Hughes: Let's recap: Human-centric mindset, agile mindset, digital-first mindset, highly influential problem solver, creativity, storytelling, networker, and social media advocate, to name a few.

When you put all the above together, the HR professional will need to embrace the combination of technologies and solutions to improve roles and work. They can drive engagement by using personas to deliver personalisation at scale and create smarter, more relevant insights to improve the end-user experience. We know that Generative AI can replicate rules-based human actions and the automation of transaction processing. These applications are already being used and continue to evolve. They can be deployed in new ways to perform higher-order activities beyond the transactional.

The HR teams are elevated by their collaboration with new machine co-workers. Equipping leaders with insights through the human-machine partnership can accelerate decision-making on some of the most complex challenges organisations face today, ranging from inclusion to equity to performance and well-being across all categories of the workforce.

Jeremy Blain and Dr Rochelle Haynes: You have mentioned the digital thread and HR 4.0 a few times. In your experience, how much of a knowledge gap is there within traditional HR in terms of digital adoption and proactively driving the use of appropriate digital tools to glue the organisation and its workforce together?

Linda Hughes: Yes, there has been a golden digital thread throughout our conversation. My slight fear is not the speed at which the technology is being developed and implemented; it is the change in control and ownership. For example, will HR professionals be confident to release some of their responsibilities to automation and trust the outcomes, and will managers be happy to implement the decisions? Yes, this is a big change, and culturally, we can't afford to hang around testing it for too long. The business imperatives require HR to move on to new roles and challenges; here are a couple of examples:

- Identifies opportunities, designs approaches, and deploys solutions using automation, robotics, cognitive, and Generative AI to augment services and solutions' effectiveness, efficiency, and data leverage.

- Embraces a digital world with the capability to envision and build new business models, tools, and ways of working informed by digital applications.

I believe there is a gap in understanding what the above two examples mean and how they could be developed. We are in danger of setting ourselves up for a fall if the market does not address this learning need – I do not see the CIPD (Chartered Institute of Personnel and Development) focusing on this as critically as they should. But it's also at the organisational level that there is a need to join up thinking across the business and function. Understanding customer data, employee data, management data and more should be a preoccupation for each function and the leaders therein. This is the power of data and supporting digital tools to bring everyone together in a way that hasn't happened before. Particularly when we now consider hybrid working, a more dispersed working population, and the rise of the blended workforce. Whole business thinking is fuelled by the consistency of digital inputs, outputs, tools, and techniques to get to the human centre of things internally and externally.

Jeremy Blain and Dr Rochelle Haynes: So, with that in mind, and with a workforce shift to manage and potentially a new HR business partnering model to pioneer, when we consider a more blended workforce, what are the risks if HR professionals don't change, don't recognise the shift; don't adapt their own Human Capital Framework, and don't advise their business leaders, particularly of this dramatic shift in workforce mix?

Linda Hughes: They are not going to be here in the future. So, the magnitude of the need to change is huge. It is a much bigger risk for a traditional human capital expert or HR professional if they cannot advise the C-Suite and even the Executive Board on the future shape of the workforce, its implications and the need for decisions and actions. This should be led by skilled, knowledgeable, and dynamic HR business partners who reflect the era and who can make this happen with the support of their executive leaders and the rest of the business.

If none of this is realised or flagged and not led by HR, then there's a massive risk that talent will not be attracted to the business, and existing talent will leave their organisation because it's not an environment they are looking to stay in. This is starting to happen in many organisations. Engagement is starting to fall, productivity is dropping, digital transformation is slowing, and financial performance is at risk. And if that is at too high a risk, it becomes a disruptor, impacting all parts of the business, including its people.

So, if executive leaders and HR business partners don't start to think about an evolved organisation framework and even business model, then they risk impacting people first, and that starts to hit the numbers, external partners, customers and more. This means that we cannot attract new people to the business and can't retain our best talents. It is my view that HR should lead this agenda, and therefore, many HR professionals at all levels need the skill sets to be able to lead, manage the tougher conversations, be data-driven and be more collaborative across the organisation.

Jeremy Blain and Dr Rochelle Haynes: In response to this, what are the most important skills, based on your experience and observations, which will benefit HR professionals, particularly senior HR professionals, in leading the organisational structure and people agenda alongside and at the heart of the executive leadership team?

Linda Hughes: The modern and complex challenges call for HR to embrace a different, more progressive way of working that builds shared value for the business, end customer, and employee. They need to start talking to people and not be bogged down again!

I would focus on reframing how HR operates fundamentally - what the right HR operating model and organisational framework is to ensure that leaders own HR 4.0. Because static frameworks of HR "best practices" and "one-size-fits" are rapidly becoming outdated. Being at the heart of business decision-making and expanding their focus across multiple stakeholders can ensure implementation of HR 4.0 by talking about how people drive business value and how HR helps to maximise that value – that means prioritising key conversations, being bold and framing the questions that provide insight to how the C-suite are prepared for the HR 4.0 challenges. The second part is working with the HR team to develop their understanding of HR 4.0 and how they want the workforce to think, feel and act - realising that 'one-size-fits-one' is just the start of the journey. When thinking about products, they have different starting points, as product design is about the end user.

Overall, HR can create a new framework, but it's the business leaders and managers that have to sponsor it, deliver it and successfully implement it, with the rest of the organisation supported by strong HR business partners.

Jeremy Blain and Dr Rochelle Haynes: It also sounds like HR business partners need to adapt their language to the stakeholders, and they will need to actively engage, mobilise, and manage as they lead the action. Would you agree?

Linda Hughes: Yes, I do. It's a good point not to use exclusively HR jargon and language. We talk about diversity in thinking and doing, and I also think we need diversity in engagement and language. We need to be able to talk finance language, sales language, marketing, leadership suite language and more. Many of my industry colleagues will need to fine-tune these skills as they simply haven't been practised enough over the last decade or so. Particularly as in some organisations, our function has increasingly pushed to the margins and become more administrative.

Jeremy Blain and Dr Rochelle Haynes: So, let's assume we've got HR professionals who've stepped up; they are around the executive leader table, they're driving the agenda, and they are holding other leaders to account in the business. What will the organisation gain by HR business partners stepping up in this way?

Linda Hughes: First, it is about HR and other leaders creating the conditions to allow people to solve problems, generate new ideas and get involved. It's not about having policies, procedures, and a tight organisation because you don't grow people in that environment. It's a situation that many companies have found themselves in, and HR professionals have been struggling to change.

So, by HR business partners stepping up this way, we accelerate progress. They lead the agenda in creating a culture that allows people to grow, be more creative and innovative, and quickly be upskilled to succeed as the business goes forward. Whether they are permanent employees or independent workers, I call it the commercialisation of HR. It's about the business imperatives through our people, who are enabled to contribute correctly across the broader workforce.

Jeremy Blain and Dr Rochelle Haynes: This helps us look at organisational development more holistically. An underpinning structure and much broader re-education in knowledge, skills and behaviour terms across HR, Talent, Learning and Development, Executive leaders and line managers and the broader workforce. So, HR leaders, business partners, and managers have to do this.

Linda Hughes: Yes. HR builds a new mindset and leads others through the process at all levels across the blended workforce, whether permanent, independent, part-time, contractor, or whatever. Once we deal with the mindset challenge, the desire for new experiences increases, and new ways of working and new dimensions are created across our multidimensional workforce. Previous anxieties, challenges, and ways of working start to evaporate and are replaced by a more positive environment fuelled by positive attitudes and ways of working. Right across the organisation. In addition, the flow and the speed by which the organisation changes will be more pronounced.

Chapter 2

OPENHR

We have discussed what is changing and why it is changing, and we must follow that up with where many new strategies fail. The how-to. Successful implementation is key, but it is difficult because there is no blueprint for structuring, supporting, and managing a truly blended workforce.

Therefore, as the authors of this book, we built a how-to blueprint from the ground up, and it seems fitting that the end result is a new home for HR to create in organisations everywhere that welcomes and supports all employees. Regardless of their designation, working preferences or location. A thoroughly modern home that is fit for purpose as we eye the 2030s and beyond.

Therefore, our OpenHR framework is imagined as a house to convey the importance of strong foundations, intentional structure, connected relationships, all-employee well-being, and a sense of belonging for permanent employees and independent contractors and workers who have a stake in creating value for the organisation.

The OpenHouse is divided into four rooms: Rules, Tools, Skills, and Thrills. Each room outlines conditions and actions needed to create the ideal work experience for different types of globally dispersed talent.

Of course, any good house is built on a solid foundation and has a leak-proof roof. It enables the whole organisation to shine and actively tackles the negativity and 'traditional mentality' lurking in the shady part of the house.

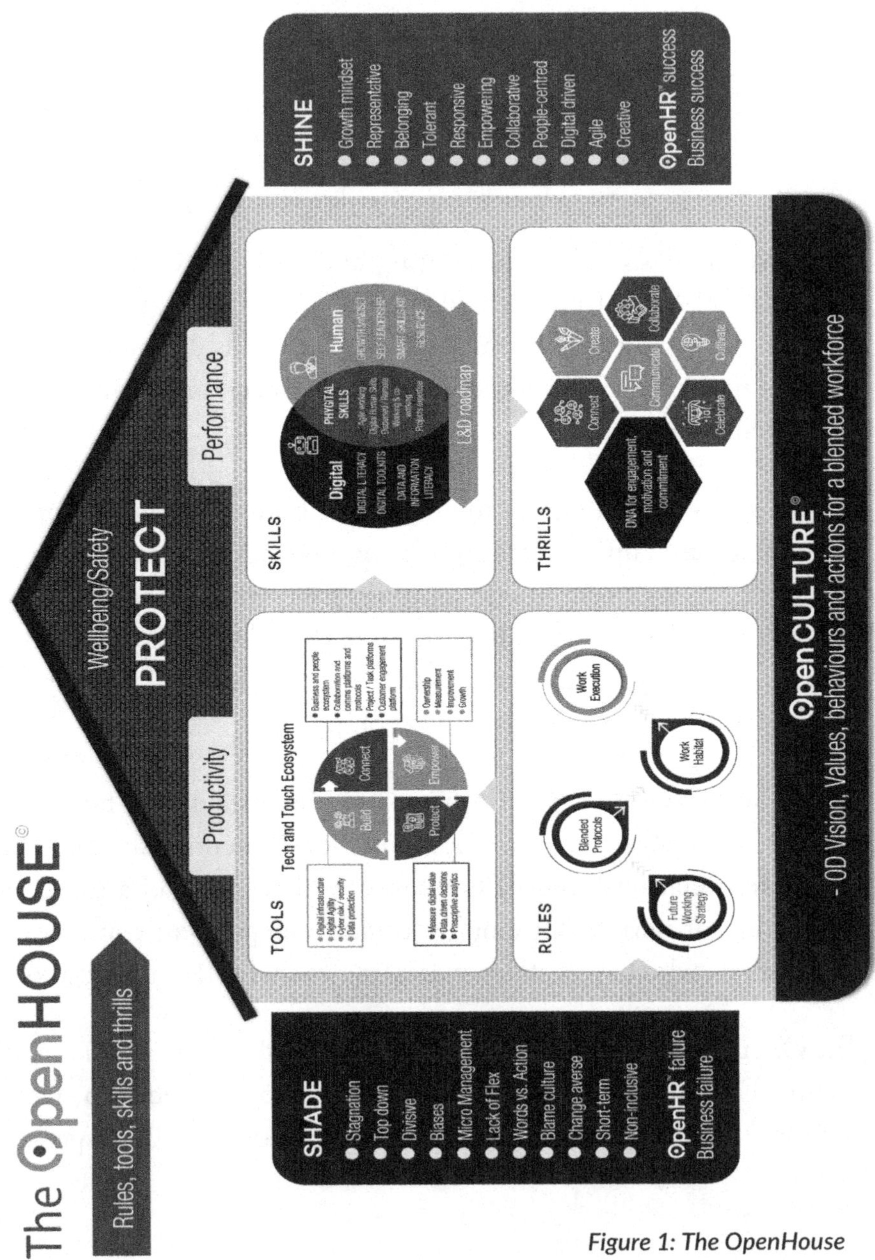

Figure 1: The OpenHouse

THE FOUR MAIN ROOMS

1. **OpenRules**: this room outlines how firms can build a work strategy that sets protocols and creates a workspace and experience suitable for the needs of different types of workers.

2. **OpenTools**: this room highlights the connected digital infrastructure needed internally to facilitate such workspaces and project execution while enabling open communication, excellence in collaboration and the delivery of excellence to the customer.

3. **OpenSkills**: this room provides a future-focused learning and development roadmap to ensure your talent is equipped with the right knowledge and skills to be effective in a constantly changing and increasingly digital business environment.

4. **OpenThrills**: this room explains how to keep your dynamic and globally dispersed talent motivated, engaged and committed to the achievement of a common goal.

These four rooms are built on the OpenCulture foundation, where the company vision and values have been communicated and agreed upon, and a strong sense of trust has been cultivated. In this vein, a sense of belonging, shared values, psychological safety, and more, are prioritised, and both permanent and independent workers model the behaviours to bind the organisation together.

The OpenHouse roof acts as a protective shield for everyone in the OpenHouse, protecting and enabling empowered work, greater collaboration, and strong management support, regardless of the designation of the various employees making up our workforce.

It also ensures we look after those operating in our house from both a physical and mental well-being perspective. A happy and healthy home.

OPENHOUSE SHADE AND SHINE

Figure 1a - Shade and Shine

Where companies get their OpenHR execution right, the positive outcomes are endless, and we list these on the sunny side of the house. It is where the organisation will **Shine**. As you can see from Figure 1a, the operational benefits are numerous as OpenHR becomes the norm, embraced by everyone.

In addition, there are strategic benefits to consider on top:

- A more flexible workforce

- Higher levels of engagement and worker satisfaction

- A larger availability of global expertise and talent

- Greater empowerment and experimentation

- Decentralised decision making

- Horizontal management structures

- Performance support vs. performance supervision

- A more diverse talent pool

- High-impact collaboration and open communication internally and across the blended workforce

- Meaningful work for permanent and independent workers

Where management continues to ignore the growing strategic importance of the open workforce and fails to prepare adequately, the results can be disastrous for businesses in this disruptive age. Our OpenHouse is in **Shade**, and the operational, day-to-day aspects are listed to the left of the OpenHouse. In addition, there are important longer term, strategic downsides that need to be considered:

- Inability to attract and retain top talent.

- Conflict in work expectations

- Misalignment of values

- Regarding the open workforce as merely managed services

- Stuck in the past rather than leading the future.

- Unattractive rather than attractive employer brand and reputation

- Legal challenges and reputational loss

- Stifled creativity

The following chapters will explore the four rooms of the OpenHR framework in more depth and will explain how both companies and their increasingly dynamic workforce can benefit from implementing its various elements.

Chapter 3

OPENCULTURE: BUILDING THE FOUNDATION

OPENCULTURE - EVERY HOUSE NEEDS A SOLID FOUNDATION

Open CULTURE©

- OD Vision, Values, behaviours and actions for a blended workforce

Figure 2: The Foundation - OpenCulture

Culture is the beginning, the middle, and the end, highlighting that it is the culture of any organisation, of any size, in any industry, which will ultimately enable success. Decades later, Peter Drucker's sentiment still rings true, regardless of how clear, effective and actionable a strategy may be or how competent a leadership team might appear. Without a good culture, then engaging permanent and independent workers as a cohesive, collaborative force becomes extremely difficult to pull off.

So, what is Culture? While there is no one agreed definition, we agree with Richard Perrin, who states:

'Organizational culture is the sum of values and rituals which serve as 'glue' to integrate the members of the organization.'[13]

Good Culture comes into sharp focus again within our OpenHR framework as we consider a diverse, equitable and inclusive organisational culture that includes permanent employees, permanent part-time employees, independent workers, and long-term contractors. And perhaps even other external stakeholders who may become central to success (for example, business partners, channel operators, and so on).

This is at the heart of our bold, new manifesto to shake up human resources management and bring together Organisation Development (OD), Human Resources (HR), talent leaders and learning professionals to champion an evolved organisational culture that is appropriate and attractive for the modern workplace and workforce.

In the 2020 article by The Alternative Board, '"Culture Eats Strategy for Breakfast" (Quoting Peter Drucker's famous saying) – What Does it Mean?,' the authors point out the symbiotic relationship between strategy implementation and culture when transforming our organisations: '…In a perfect scenario, culture and strategy complement and nurture each other. Strategy and culture should be created simultaneously, making sure they are perfectly aligned. When in sync, they enable each other to create incredible organisational transformations.'[14]

---

13   https://hbr.org/2013/05/what-is-organizational-culture

14   https://www.thealternativeboard.com/blog/culture-eats-strategy

This is how strategy and culture become inseparable. Culture informs and underpins an appropriate strategy – in terms of how it is defined and then, importantly, how it is executed with everyone involved. The two work together in alignment with organisational values and behaviours as central pillars, embraced from the bottom up as well as the top down.

WHAT DOES CULTURE LOOK LIKE IN THE OPENHR ERA?

There are two considerations driving the need for an evolved company culture:

1. **All organisations are going through a transformational shift.** Culture includes digital, business, workforce, distributed working, redefined business models and the need for a more human-centred leadership, one that balances people with profit and purpose.

2. **The rise of the open economy and the blended workforce:** not only do we need a human resources framework and culture appropriate for a blend of permanent and independent workers, but we also need it for evolved business models like hybrid working, flexible working and 100% distributed working.

In this respect, culture has been ready for an upgrade for some time, and it is the enlightened organisations, evolving for the modern workplace, who are leading the way. For example, Southwest Airlines, Four Seasons Group, Spotify, DBS Bank, Telstra, WordPress, JLL and more.

There is a good mix of more traditional organisations now thinking like 21st-century businesses and a new era of companies built on and fuelled by digital technologies and progress while mastering the human touch. It can be achieved in two ways: the first is at the organisation level, and the second is at the team level.

This is particularly important due to increasingly remote, dispersed teams collaborating largely online. Therefore, reinforcing the main company culture with a strong team culture built on solid values and behaviours will mobilise, engage, motivate and accelerate great co-working as much as excellence individually.

At both organisation and team level, one question is a good place to start:

What are the values and behaviours that will underpin our culture change so that we all thrive in this new era?

A thriving blended workforce culture is one that is adaptable and responsive to the opportunities, threats and challenges presented by technology, the disruption of markets, changing customer behaviours, the evolving workforce mix and changing ways of working. With a blended and distributed workforce, it is the blend of the digital and the human touch that will be paramount to achieving the necessary cultural shift.

Companies who are championing culture as central to the modern workplace – at both team and organisation levels – include Your FLOCK, the UK tech company that provides a mobile-first platform to assess, build and support culture shift based on values and behaviours central to the most successful companies globally, or customised to suit.[15]

---

15   http://www.yourflock.co.uk

Another company that is taking organisational culture evolution to another level is www.happily.ai, co-founded by the Jafferi brothers in Thailand.[16] Happily.ai transforms work environments and cultures from being disconnected to measurably engaged with real-time data and AI, making performance, feedback, and recognition daily habits. This is how to measure cultural evolution and health on an ongoing, daily, unremitting basis. Because it is that important to business health, workforce engagement and overall growth.

These new breeds of companies are pioneering an 'agile culture shift' – which recognises that in the rapidly changing workplace and the acceleration of the blended workforce, culture needs to adapt and evolve at the same rate. This means that culture can be subtly tweaked and modified to suit the organisation, different teams and new expectations while protecting the company's cultural heart.

In the Forbes article '*16 Strategies for Building a Positive Culture with Onsite and Freelance Talent*,' Forbes Business Council members gave their advice for building and enhancing culture for a blended workforce, when permanent workers rub shoulders with independent workers both in the office and virtually.[17] Their tips flow from leaning into synergies and evolving a more adaptable culture, with values that recognise contribution can come from the whole workforce, not just permanent workers within the company walls.

Therefore, once culture and values for the modern, more fluid workplace and workforce have been established, it is about putting in place the operational actions that allow everyone to 'walk the walk' in cultural terms (at all levels) as much as 'talk the talk.' These are the critical components to accelerate success.

---

16   www.happily.ai

17   https://www.forbes.com/councils/forbesbusinesscouncil/2021/10/22/16-strategies-for-building-a-positive-culture-with-onsite-and-freelance-talent/

Take a moment to consider your organisation's culture and the immediate points that come to mind, both positive and developmental, to help you capture early thoughts around how you might reignite Culture building or evolution in your space:

We need to stop doing	We need to continue doing	We need to start doing

Our culture – now and moving forward.
(make notes to capture ideas and actions)

Immediate big wins	
Immediate risks to mitigate.	
Benefits we can realise.	

BUILDING YOUR OPENCULTURE

Questions and actions to work through

In order to make progress, you may need to have a high-level discussion across functions and at the executive leader level to work through how organisational culture evolves when we consider all the transformations that may need to be tackled. For example, digital, the blended workforce, the hybrid workplace, adopting Agile ways of working, Diversity, Equity, and Inclusion (DE&I) requirements, shifting employee expectations, customer loyalty drivers and more.

The following questions can be used as they are and in full or as a menu of options to start conversations around the most important cultural aspects of your organisation's evolution and on the central components critical to culture change for a blended workforce.

Alongside this, we will provide questions that recognise the need for 'digital glue' as much as the human component, considering the role of technology in business and as an enabler of the multi-dimensional workforce. In fact, these three associated links will help demonstrate the importance of the digital thread in building a more stable and modern organisational culture. A useful pause for reflection before you get into the questions.

One study to look through: https://www.mckinsey.com/capabilities/mckinsey-digital/our-insights/culture-for-a-digital-age. Here, McKinsey shows that the number one most significant challenge to meeting digital priorities is squarely around culture and behaviours.

Insights to learn from: https://jdmeier.com/how-to-create-a-digital-culture-in-your-organization

One podcast to tune in to: 'The importance of adopting a Transformational Culture Model'

With David Liddle. Hosted by Jeremy Blain as part of his 'Rethink Leadership' podcast series.[18]

---

18   https://shorturl.at/nvAJO

POWERING UP AN OPENCULTURE

Questions to accelerate the conversation and to move forward

Key Questions	Notes and Ideas	Your 90-Day Action Plan
Considering where we are now and where we want to be in the decade ahead, what does our gold standard organisation culture look & feel like for an increasingly digital environment?		
What are the values and behaviours that will underpin our culture change so that we all thrive in this new era?		
How do we build organisational culture from the ground up rather than top-down?		

Equity, diversity, and inclusion are key to attracting, growing and retaining a powerful workforce – how do we ensure this is at the heart of an evolved culture?		
Blended workforce and blended working: How does our culture embrace and drive a sense of belonging for all stakeholders, whether permanent employees, remote workers, independent workers, contractors, traditional workers, or digital workers?		
How will we define and explain our evolved culture internally and externally?		

How will our culture reflect a modern approach to business stewardship, balancing people, purpose, and profit?		
How will prospective employees (whether permanent or independent resources) view our organisation's culture?		
How will our partners and customers view our organisation's culture?		
What is the cost of not evolving or adapting our culture to the times?		

What other organisations do we admire, and what can we learn from their company culture?		
What organisations have failed in their cultural evolution and focus that we can also learn from?		
Who could advise us (externally and internally) and feed in emerging best practices/case studies to help us shape our journey and outputs?		

How do we start a 90-day roadmap with the support of executive leaders and our workforce? Who can we include in our project team to drive the journey of culture evolution as representatives of all the stakeholders we have discussed above?		
Specifically, how do we build into our culture DNA a strong sense of belonging for independent workers and contractors?		

How will we manage and measure the impact of our culture in both qualitative and quantitative dimensions? • At the organisational level? • At function/ team / work-group level?		
How do we create a digitally driven ecosystem to enhance communication, collaboration and bold empowerment across our evolving workforce?		

In the modern, ever-changing workplace, Culture will eat strategy for breakfast, lunch, and dinner unless it becomes the heartbeat of the organisation. Keeping it fit, healthy, adaptable and suited to modern business is essential – whether people are permanent workers of independent contractors, whether they are office-based or remote, whether they are in your country of operations or more dispersed, whether they are technologically brilliant or traditional workers; whether they are young or experienced; whether they are management or individual contributors; whether they are male or female; and whether they are from different countries and cultures.

Building your OpenCulture is action one, step one in your journey to building the OpenHouse - It is the most solid of foundations when done right. It can slip, slide, and crumble if it is not.

Chapter 4

OPENRULES:
THE FIRST ROOM

Figure 3 - OpenRules

Freelancers represent a talent group that companies can no longer afford to ignore. There has been a steady rise globally in independent or gig work, as many people seek out more flexibility and autonomy in their work lives. For companies, gig workers create the opportunity to hire 'expertise on tap,' reduce fixed costs, and offer numerical flexibility. A 2022 study in the USA found that there are nearly 59 million workers in the U.S. who are classified as independent workers - equating to 36 percent of the U.S. workforce[19]. Comparatively, around 100 million workers are classified as permanent workers.

As the volume of these workers increases, companies must create an organisational environment that considers and caters to different work approaches. During our study, an HR Director at a top global IT firm shared that many of the brightest female talents do not want to work on a full-time basis. Contrary to popular belief, this is not only due to childcare needs but instead shifting ideas and reshaping perspectives around how work should be experienced. While flexitime and job rotations have provided some adaptability in the past, many workers expressed that they are not interested in being in these arrangements.

An evolving workforce demands new rules and protocols. The OpenRules room is focused on helping firms create an open talent strategy that sets protocols and creates workspaces and experiences suitable for the needs of both the organisation and its various types of workers. These rules are in alignment with the initialised OpenCulture and, as this develops, become an embedded way of initialising and engaging your blended workforce. The above diagram highlights the four central elements needed to achieve this, which will be discussed in more detail in this chapter:

1. Future working strategy

2. Blended protocols

3. Work experience

4. Work habitat

---

19   https://www.mckinsey.com/featured-insights/sustainable-inclu-
      sive-growth/future-of-america/freelance-side-hustles-and-gigs-many-
      more-americans-have-become-independent-workers

Therefore, our main goal when considering the 'Rules' room is:

To understand the roadblocks in attracting and engaging both the blend of permanent (in-house) and independent talent and to create an organisational roadmap for the future that allows firms to leverage the strategic value of all of their people.

Our OpenRules component parts will also guide companies on how to create an environment of belonging and inclusion for their diversified and dispersed talent pool. This includes considering what protocols and people management adjustments and tools are needed to create a work environment that can accommodate different types of talent, including open talent.

The OpenRules room is arguably the most critical to get right. This is nothing short of remodelling the HR framework from how we used to manage human capital, to a reimagining of what is required and possible. In our work, this has resulted in a brand-new framework for a blended workforce. Future-proofing talent attraction, growth and retention at a time when competition for all talent designations is at its highest for over a decade.

The OpenRules Key Questions to respond to prior to accelerating actions:

- What is HR's role in creating an agile organisational environment that is fit for the blended workforce?

- What are the organisational rules and procedures that are needed to engage a blended workforce effectively?

- How do companies create a future work strategy that allows them to leverage different types of talent according to different organisational needs?

- How do we create an organisational environment that is attractive and accommodating to open talent and blended work teams?

- How do we create an empowered, open workforce that is able to work collaboratively in the execution of tasks, targets, projects, and all-level innovation and problem-solving?

The Benefits of responding to these questions up front:

- Increased organisational clarity, reduced sunk costs, boosted efficiency and collaborative effectiveness across all resources, and worked more strategically in a high-performing global talent pool.

- Developing the right infrastructure for your blended team also opens the door for companies to attract, grow, reward, and retain a wider group of talent globally, including expert and highly skilled freelancers. This, in turn, ensures the organisation is embracing and recognising the benefits of a diversity of thinking, as well as the benefits of a truly diverse workforce and the richness that it can bring, whether that is around an increase in underrepresented, marginalised groups, neurodivergent talent, differently-abled talent, and globally dispersed migrants and refugees who have been displaced but may come with serious credentials, perfect for your challenges.

- Less focus on 'fitting into a mould.' With the level of uncertainty, speed of transformational need, new competition, digital innovation and more, the need for 'differences are good' thinking should come to the fore.

The watch outs:

- Being too legalistic and taking a transactional approach to engagement with open talent. Assuming that all groups of workers want the same thing. Available talent may choose to work with one of your competitors, which recognises the strength in diversity we are arguing for.

- Secondly, organisations should be conscious of not treating the independent workforce too casually or as merely a convenience. It's a new mindset. We need a mindset where we value all employees, regardless of their designation, and that must come with new values and behaviours modelled from the top of the organisation and through every level.

THE OPENHR CHALLENGE

- To create an environment where companies can truly leverage the value of different types of talent and where freelancers and other forms of open talent feel considered and included in a structured and thoughtful way.

- To develop a work ecosystem that is equipped with the right support and protocols to guide and boost the confidence of leaders and hiring managers who seek to engage different types of talent effectively.

THE OPENRULES ROOM AS A WHOLE:

Since the Second Industrial Revolution, businesses have promoted and operated within a nine-to-five model of work, which primarily utilised full-time, in-house employees. However, technological advancements, shifting priorities, work expectations, the availability of greater connectivity, and more, are leading businesses to rethink long-held ideas about how work should be organised and the most productive way of getting things done for the benefit of customers, with an engaged workforce fully on board. This is the open secret in attracting and engaging the best-emerging talent across the globe. Now, more and more individuals are looking for flexibility, meaningful work, challenge, enjoyment, and fulfilment.

When it comes to becoming ready for the future, organisations are running out of time. A 2023 study by MBO Partners showed that digital nomadism in the US increased by 131% between 2019 and 2022[20].

Since then, their latest Digital Nomadism Report has shown that this type of location-independent work has now crossed over into the mainstream. Another recent study by Gallup in 2023[21], stated:

"Employees in the U.S. continued to feel more detached from their employers, with less clear expectations, lower levels of satisfaction with their organisation, and less connection to its mission or purpose, than they did four years ago. They are also less likely to feel someone at work cares about them as a person."

This should be a wake-up call for all business leaders, as Gallup also observed in the same article that this low engagement was

20   https://www.mbopartners.com/state-of-independence/digital-nomads/

21   https://www.gallup.com/workplace/608675/new-workplace-employ-ee-engagement-stagnates.aspx

costing the US economy **about $1.9 trillion in lost productivity;** and that what was needed to improve this was a change in the way companies managed their people. In the US alone, talent attrition costs companies up to 500 million USD in annual expenditure.

Coming out of the COVID-19 pandemic of the early 2020s, stress levels of employees globally were at an all-time high, and as a result, many were more demanding of better work environments and increased flexibility, leading them to pursue freelancing as an alternative to full-time employment. The problem remains, however, that most companies, in mindset and infrastructure, are still outfitted to primarily accommodate full-time staff in a more traditional 20th-century model without considering the best structure for an ever-evolving, digitally enabled 21st-century workplace.

The resultant need is to create a work environment where companies can easily operationalise different approaches to working and different types of talent and where these various groups feel recognised, supported, and valued when companies engage them.

Within the current context, many leaders view changing work demands as a 'remote vs. non-remote work' debate, but that was never the core issue. It isn't about the former versus the latter but rather about making different work options available and empowering organisational stakeholders to engage with a wider array of talent and expertise. This is where the OpenRules come in.

Let's start with perceptions. Many organisations are missing the bigger picture when seeking to use open talent. Unfortunately, despite growing numbers and changing worker demands, freelancers or independent contractors are still viewed as casual add-ons rather than key contributors to the organisations' strategic objectives. Even where some firms acknowledge this contribution, their treatment of freelancers paints a different, less flattering picture. Employers often hire open talent, then take an 'out of sight, out of mind' attitude towards these key stakeholders. Reasons for this include the lack of physical presence, as well as compliance concerns. Within the US, for example, too much engagement with freelancers means that there is a risk of misclassification, which presents all kinds of compliance and legal anxiety for organisations. Cautionary tales like the Uber Supreme Court ruling (Uber BV v Aslam, 2021[22]) highlighted the ramifications of treating an independent contractor like a full-time employee. Attempting to set freelancers' wages, onboarding, and training, as well as too much engagement by companies, could result in large fines.

However, instead of shrinking their talent pool by avoiding the inevitable increased engagement with open talent, companies need to understand their level of responsibility to specific types of talent when creating their future workforce strategy. Moreover, if they are using an intermediary to hire talent (e.g., an open talent or 'gig' platform or outsource agent), then they should also understand what level of responsibility these external stakeholders hold. A critical part of this is being able to distinctively define different types of open talent and clearly articulate the type of work that freelancers are being asked to perform.

INTERVIEW WITH ERYN PETERS, FOUNDER AND CEO OF THE STARTUP CONSORTIUM

To better understand organisational challenges with engaging open talent and how these are being addressed, we spoke with Eryn Peters, futurist and founder of the Weekly Workforce and StartUp Consortium. This boutique consulting firm helps startups and remote organisations achieve hypergrowth. Eryn is also the US Director of

---

22   https://www.wainwrightcummins.co.uk/site/blog/firm-news/
      uber-bv-v-aslam-case-summary

the Association for the Future of Work. Here are the key extracts from our chat:

Jeremy Blain and Dr Rochelle Haynes: What do you see as the key reasons that companies seek to engage with open talent in your experience?

Eryn: Among the main reasons to open jobs to freelancers is where you need to move faster or expand your team. You might just need more bandwidth or very specialised skills for something that's a one-off. You might hire a freelancer to fix this one thing, and then your normal team can take things over. There's something to be said about bringing in external background and experience and different ways to diversify ways of thinking or diversified ways of working. There's also added value in having someone be neutral or impartial for things like audits. Sometimes, you do want a third party to come in and look at things of that nature. And the other reason is also to be able to bypass certain hiring things and hire from other regions. For example, maybe I want to hire someone from Southeast Asia because I'm working on a project with a client who needs to know how to write in a certain style of writing, which was a situation that we had in the past. There's a customer who was looking for someone who spoke Arabic, and they needed a UX UI designer because they were going to have their website in both English and Arabic. And obviously, one reads left to right, and one reads right to left. So, having someone who had a design way of thinking and had been exposed to it on a regular basis was super important. This was going to be a long-term, ongoing type of role and relationship. But they couldn't really find someone who had that niche expertise within their own region. And they almost had to hire on a contract basis, even though they wanted this person long-term, because they didn't have an entity where this person was located in the Middle East. So that hits a number of boxes where you can't find something locally, or you can't find a perfect fit.

Jeremy Blain and Dr Rochelle Haynes: That's a great example. And what role does language play in your experience and your engagement with freelancers and clients? What language do they typically use to describe different groups of talent, and how does that define the organisation's engagement with them?

Eryn: I think using contingent portrays freelancers or open talent like a backup or contingency plan. It makes it seem like these workers are coming in as second-class citizens. It can also make your own team feel like they're not good enough because you need to bring in someone to save the day. For those organisations who are doing it well, it's not a backup plan. It's their first plan. It's how they strategically implement talent in different ways, shapes and forms. It's a way of hiring someone to come in and provide that surgical fix when needed but then having a long-term team that carries things through. So, I hate the word contingent workforce because I think it's better suited to normalise strategic or blended workforces, where you have different contract types and different ways of working.

I think there's also a big difference when you say terms like 'remote-friendly' versus 'remote-first.' The way that people behave and the way that people allow certain things or have preconceptions of certain things are very different within a remote-first environment. This means that if one person is not in the room for the meeting, we all take the meeting on Zoom to our desk on our own computer because it levels the playing field. If it's remote, then it's ten of us in a conference room with one speaker, and it's still an awful experience for the remote person. That person never gets to chime in and is often excluded by others. But to most, that's usually okay because they are present at the meeting.

However, the way in which they behave is still remote; for example, they can be at home picking up the kids. So, I think the way that you behave in a remote-first or remote-okay organisation is quite different. And I think that when we talk about change within organisations, there's also a difference between 'remote native' companies and 'remote transitioned' companies and how much they've developed these types of muscles. And I do believe that a lot more remote global workers and contractors, by nature, have 'remote-native' best practices.

That's because knowledge workers in other parts of the world have worked remotely much longer than companies that are just starting to transition and are used to doing a lot of things off-site. But now, suddenly, you have people around the world that are working on these teams. This can also make hybrid work the hardest environment to work in because of that. For example, most companies haven't really defined what counts as a hybrid experience. Whether it's on-site or remote, we are still figuring out what type of hybrid model is being used. Is it hybrid in the sense of 'This week, we all need to be in this one spot?' Or is it hybrid in the sense that 90% of the time, we're remote, and then one week, a year, one week, a quarter, we all get together somewhere in the world, and we actually work on-site because, to me, that's also hybrid? I think those are some of the nuances that determine whether we are 'remote-native' versus 'remote-transitioned' or 'remote-friendly' versus remote-first.

Jeremy Blain and Dr Rochelle Haynes: This is absolutely fascinating. I just want to go back to a couple of things you said there. So, for example, you mentioned remote best practices. Can you give me some examples of remote native best practices versus remote transition practices?

Eryn: Absolutely. So even down to something as silly and nuanced as file-sharing. A remote-native company has always had things in a digital environment where policies, procedures, and things we've documented are typically stored in some digital file place. They've probably had only one tool that they've used, for example, Google Docs or Teams. It's not a mix of people from different offices at different times who have done different things or have SharePoint or similar mechanisms. So remote-native companies are very knowledgeable about these kinds of digital tools because there is no other option. It is all online. So, they're using recorded meetings, and they're already working across time zones, both synchronously and asynchronously.

Asynchronous is a lot better in remote-native teams because, from day one, that's what they've been working with. When you have remote-transitioned, especially groups that are now multinational or are just now getting familiar with a hybrid type of environment, you're always going to find that the people who were already working on-site possess a lot more tribal knowledge because I can just quickly tell you that a coffee across the street, and that's very normal.

They rely on things like learning by osmosis more because you can just sit next to someone and shadow them. And there's a general lack of intention to make things that way because of the ease and convenience of someone who's next to you, so they don't have that muscle of going.

Remote workers don't get that experience because they're not like they are in the same location. Companies often don't really don't know how to replicate that in ways that are effective because their people are just inherently comfortable with what they're used to, so convenience and intention are some of the bigger ones, even when it comes down to building relationships.

People who have been remote-native or remote for a long time have a good muscle for reaching out to people just to say hey and hang out.

Otherwise, you only talk to someone when you need something from them. And I find people who are new to remote work environments don't do that. Because they forget about you unless you're there, because that's how that's what they're used to, if I see you, then I'll chat with you.

But otherwise, I'm really just going to reach out when I need something. So, like passive versus active, and it's a level of intent, I think, there have been general observations of different orcs as they've transitioned.

Jeremy Blain and Dr Rochelle Haynes: Okay, so what do you see as the organisation's future workforce needs? And how can different types of talent be leveraged?

Eryn: I think roles today even are kind of silly and outdated. This is why a lot of people need 'contingent' workers; their roles are out of date. There's never someone who has 100% of the qualifications for a role that's listed. So, you're not hiring what you thought that you needed in any way. You can ask any manager that's hired about the number of times they've found someone that goes, and you're not fit for this job. But actually, you should do this other thing. And by the time people come in, especially in fast-paced environments, by the time anything happens, people and their interests have changed.

The role didn't fully describe what their job was going to be, so they're actually doing something quite different. The company has grown so significantly that their roles have changed; they've re-organised and done a million different things. And now they're going, "What am I going to do with this person that I hired? That's a startup narrow generalist, but now I need a specialist, so what do I do with them now?" It's going to be too expensive to keep them up to date and all this stuff, so basically, roles are just not descriptive, not the right fit, and not future proof. So, if we start thinking of things less as roles and more of the skill application or project application of work, then what's great is now you have a bunch of employees that move and transition freely, which is much more attractive to young workers these days, as well as they want to move around within organisations. Even if it is a horizontal move, they want to see different departments; they want to try new things, like the diversification of tasks.

Employment is such an important part of learning, growing, and earning more money as you jump around to different things. But if we can basically move away from roles and move towards projects and skills, then contingent workers fit within that so much nicer.

Most companies operate like an agency because they have this thing that needs to be done. And I'm going to get people who have the skills to do that thing. And when that thing is over, I'm going to have people who have the skills to maintain that thing. And realistically, that's also matching with people's desires. I'm a builder; I'm not an optimizer. I want to come in when everything is burning, and on the ground, I want to put some structure in place. But I don't want to optimise the marketing campaign for an extra 0.8 per cent. I don't think the world is ready for this. We're nowhere near being ready for this.

And you have companies like Bubty, for example, that are trying to build internal talent pools to do this, at least to manage contracting freelancers. But roles are just such a thing of the past because nobody's actually investing to make them work. And that's where we're getting a lot of employee turnover.

Employee tenure is at an all-time low right now, especially if we take industry; it's like 18 months to maybe two years in the place versus the 20 to 30 years of the past. Young workers want diversity, young workers want people to invest in them and all these other things, and now they're ready to be like, "F*ck it, I'm going to go do another project that values my skills." This is true, especially when we talk about Gen Z and millennials because this is what they want.

Conclusion

The above highlights the need to start thinking about using different types of talent from the very beginning or as a re-engineered talent management approach rather than reactively filling arising skills gaps, as is typically done by most organisations.

Eryn also shed light on what many companies have realised in the last ten years: that traditional approaches or organising work and outlining jobs may no longer be best for achieving the strategic outcomes desired by leaders and attracting the talent most capable of delivering on these outcomes. Creating an environment where different types of talent feel challenged, appreciated and respected for their contribution is imperative if companies want to benefit from a more inclusive and innovative workforce. While the word 'inclusive' creates some more compliance-related fears, these risks can be reduced by implementing a comprehensive talent framework like OpenHR.

In our OpenRules quadrants, we outline key considerations for developing a blended workforce and clear guidelines for integrating freelancers into the existing organisational ecosystem.

OPENRULES COMPONENT BY COMPONENT

In our first room, OpenRules, we unlock the keys to truly leveraging your blended workforce. We do this by offering firms a strategic road map and key protocols for engaging independent workers and integrating them into their organisational workforce. Having discussed the key challenges involved in engaging open talent, along with the core issues companies should be addressing to alleviate specific fears, we will outline our five OpenRules component parts below.

1. FUTURE WORKING STRATEGY

It is time for companies to work less transactionally and more effectively and strategically with their blended teams. Managing your blended workforce more effectively requires foresight in understanding and accommodating the needs of the various groups of talent in your project team before reaching the point of conflict, miscommunication, or unachieved objectives. For example, with a clear knowledge of when to use freelancers, how they can contribute, who the freelancer should be reporting to, how much interaction is expected, and how to source company information, organisations and their workforce can benefit from efficiency, innovation, and productivity gains. It is crucial that companies outline a clear vision of how they intend to engage more agile talent at different points in their business cycle, including the frequency and type of worker. Individuals who are more aligned with the organisation's mission and values are more likely to be committed, engaged, and productive. In addition to this, individuals should have clearly outlined goals, strategies, and success criteria that can actually be measured. The use of data can be leveraged to identify and gauge success metrics around productivity and freelancers' contributions within their respective teams.

An important finding in MBO and Partners' digital nomad study quoted above was not just that there was a 49% increase in digital nomads in 2023, but that it was largely driven by full-time employees who gave up their traditional, permanent jobs to work as independent, from anywhere[23]. This includes an increasing number of highly capable and talented Gen X'ers choosing to walk away from the corporate world, which many feel is in a transformational crisis.

If companies want to benefit from the best and brightest minds who are opting for more flexibility and a better work-life balance, then they will have to include these workers in their future work planning. To underpin these shifts, HR practitioners will also need to evolve existing policies. So, let's examine a little more closely what this might look like.

Understanding Work Arrangements: Terms of Engagement

Over the past decade, we have seen the ongoing struggle of global, regional, and national institutions and lawmakers to define freelance work and fully grasp what they need in terms of work arrangements and protections. However, there seems to be a collective awakening among various global regulators to the value that freelancers and gig

---

23   https://www.mbopartners.com/state-of-independence/digital-nomads/

workers provide as more and more leaders advocate more fiercely for protections in the gig economy.

In July 2023, China's Premier, Li Qiang, after discussions with companies including Alibaba's cloud unit, Meituan, PDD Holdings' Pinduoduo and JD.com, promised that the government would work to make platform firm regulation more transparent and predictable. Beijing changed its stance in December, emphasising the need to reinvigorate the expansive online platform sector in light of its economic contribution.

Singapore's senior minister of state for manpower, Koh Poh Koon, observed that gig workers said the pandemic had demonstrated that platform workers in the city-state provide a "useful service" and are "here to stay" for the foreseeable future and whose longer-term demands to work in this way should not be overlooked. He advocated for needs, including housing, injury compensation, and retirement security, to be taken into account as this would provide workers with some legal mandate to bargain with platform businesses on an equal footing. These remarks followed the Singapore government's acceptance of a set of suggestions made by a tripartite workgroup to ensure that platform employees were more adequately represented.

This increase in Asian authorities joining the choir of European and North American regulators could signal that a basic floor of rights for independent workers is now firmly on the agenda. Even more encouraging is regulators' openness to tripartite resolutions to create guiding mechanisms that adequately serve the varying parties concerned.

Where there is the absence of external legal apparatus that adequately defines and outlines the nature of engagement with freelancers, companies have the opportunity to step up to the mound and develop their own organisational tools.

To leverage workforce evolution and create a more relevant and timely organisation, HR needs to communicate and work closely with key stakeholders and decision-makers across the company, including finance, legal, and procurement departments, to create a systematic approach to sourcing, vetting, onboarding, and engaging, and, where necessary, integrating open talent. If this is in place from day one, clique formation, siloing, and a 'zero-sum game' attitude can be avoided. Then, we can build a truly powerful 'one team' orientation with everyone working with each other for the growth of the business.

What's more, it will develop seamless flow and cohesion by creating a sense of belonging amongst the various categories and groups of employees (freelancers and full-time employees; office-based and geographically dispersed teams and individuals). To create these tools of engagement, firms must first understand their past, present and future needs.

Leveraging your Workforce Strategy: Understanding your Talent Needs

The lack of clearly outlined rules of engagement for freelancers predates the 2020 Covid-19 pandemic, which resulted in a global uptake of remote work. A 2019 Deloitte report examining the alternative workforce highlighted that less than 10% of organisations globally have the necessary processes in place to manage their alternative workforce effectively. When we asked expert Kaumudi Goda[24] about the state of human capital management, she stated:

---

24   https://www.linkedin.com/in/kaumudi-goda

"Some people management actions needed
urgently include re-imagining the acquisition,
engagement, and retention of talent, and
thinking about rewards and benefits which are
suited to a more diversified talent pool, yet
personalised to employees' individual situations,
work contracts and job descriptions."

Developing and setting your OpenRules builds an environment that allows your full-time workforce to easily integrate independent contractors, either of whom might come and go during the lifetime of specific projects. Many digital nomads and gigsters tend to work under very informal under-the-table arrangements or travel on the 'down low' because most companies lack any formal 'work from anywhere' policies. If companies are going to engage location-independent workers meaningfully, then they must have suitable protocols that accommodate the needs of this group while protecting against compliance and other regulatory risks. To do this, a company should start with a review of existing people management policies and procedures to pinpoint the current barriers to engaging freelancers. More importantly, firms should have an acute understanding of their overall vision behind engaging different talent groups.

What's Your Why?

To achieve the above-mentioned equity and evolution of the company's workforce, companies must take time to reflect on their purpose and vision behind creating a future workforce strategy. Organisations engage freelance talent for a myriad of reasons, some including filling talent gaps, requirements for speed and agility, rapid company growth, fresh or external perspective, and or increased diversity of experiences. Hence, HR leaders must be aware of where the demand for different types of talent is coming from within the existing organisational ecosystem. One way of gaining clarity on this is to identify and analyse the existing makeup of your workforce. This means having an acute understanding of how talent is sourced and deployed across the organisation, or in other words, the 'anatomy of a hire.' To carry out this introspection, consider four key factors:

1. **The Talent Pool or Source:** E.g., Platforms, job agencies, internal talent pools, internship programs, etc.

2. **Contract / Classification Type:** E.g., Contractor (1099), Employee (W2), Agency hire, etc.

3. **Engagement / Scope:** E.g., short-term vs. long-term, project-based vs time and materials, milestones, level of project privacy and risk, etc.

4. **Payment / Fulfilment:** E.g., Vendor onboarding, PEO/EOR, payment solutions platforms, etc.

By examining the deployment of different types of talent across the company, leaders and managers gain great insight into and can better assess the requirements and strategic contribution of different types of talent. This requires a dedicated team of cross-departmental stakeholders who can act as the seat of knowledge for the company's future workforce and develop the appropriate and context-driven mechanisms for blended working. In their recent book, '*Open Talent*'[25], John Winsor and Jin H. Paik suggest that large firms with the necessary resources could establish a Center of Excellence (COE), which assembled experts from across different departments to develop tools and strategies for effective talent engagement. Through their cross-departmental collaboration, this entity could

---

25   https://a.co/d/cSGsToT

foster greater knowledge and information sharing, as well as enhance innovation within the organisation. Similarly, a blended workforce project team made up of key stakeholders would head any future workforce strategy initiative, gathering key knowledge on talent engagement, analysing past outcomes and future objectives, and using this data to gain buy-in and inform new practice. John also noted that COEs or similar ensembles could be used as a space to experiment and pilot strategies before unleashing them into the wider company context. John stressed that when companies choose this approach, choosing the right leader who could set the tone for the type of culture that the firm wants to create and who could mobilise and encourage different internal stakeholders. Given their wider resourcing and people management mandates, as well as their knowledge of and access to internal software that typically stores employees' information and employment lifecycle, we believe that HR should either lead or work in close partnership with the selected leader for this initiative. In saying this, however, we recognise that many firms do not even possess HR departments, or in other cases, the people management function is made up of a team of one. Hence, organisations need to assess their individual circumstances and needs and decide which approach would be more strategically valuable. An alternative to firms with fewer resources could be to designate or recruit a single person who concentrates on coordinating open talent (OT) and blended workforce solutions. Whichever option is pursued, the effectiveness of any COE or blended workforce strategy initiative requires close collaboration with line managers, who have a front-row seat to the firm's daily operations and can practically inform the review of existing tools and practices and the development of new rules of engagement. Also, they can explain and advise on any suggested changes that might affect existing employees and projects.

One of the key responsibilities of a company's blended workforce initiative should be to identify the existing talent streams and pipelines within the organisation and the primary purposes that they have been engaged in the past and present. While many companies question the use of open talent, different divisions and departments within the organisation are already engaging freelancers to some extent. Moreover, many company employees themselves are freelancing on the side. Hence, people management professionals should make it a priority to identify and document existing talent streams and pipelines in the organisation and understand how these different talent sources are being deployed across the organisation. With DEI at the forefront of most companies' minds, this can also help firms highlight where diverse talent streams are being accessed across the organisation. In doing this, companies can also learn about how non-traditional talent is perceived compared to full-time talent. Some key questions to ask may include:

1. Are there any existing DEI talent streams or pools?

2. How are freelancers or non-traditional talent perceived by in-house employees and management?

3. What is the balance of push and pull between managers choosing talent sources vs. recruitment/procurement choosing approved channels?

The above also emphasises the need for companies to collect data that reveals the different types of talent being used across the organisation, the contracts being used to hire non-traditional talent, the skills gaps being filled by such talent, and the various skills possessed by in-house employees (more about this in our OpenSkills chapter). In addition to identifying existing talent groups, companies should also seek to understand further workers' classification and what this means for the nature of their business interaction or working relationship. This should include, for example, whether they are operating as a limited company or as a sole trader, the current working practices used when interacting with freelancers, whether they have multiple clients and or non-compete agreements, and whether they enjoyed working with the company. Leaders must be clear about how open talent is integrated into the organisation to ensure they can successfully navigate compliance and legal requirements.

In developing your future workforce strategy, we've outlined a starter self-evaluation questionnaire that helps companies understand where they are as they venture down this new path. By answering the below questions, HR professionals can begin to identify and outline elements of the workforce anatomy and understand how they contribute strategically.

Future Workforce Strategy: Self-Evaluation Questionnaire:

Self-Evaluation Questions:	Response
What are your existing flexible arrangements and 'work from anywhere' options and policies?	
What employment classifications are currently being used within your organisation?	

What is your current hiring anatomy? For what reasons are you hiring different groups of workers?	
What current sources are being used to hire freelancers and other open talent?	
What are the main areas in which you are currently hiring open talent?	
What is the nature of engagement with open talent? E.g. Short-term or long-term? Project-related?	
How do you plan to onboard free-lancers with the rest of the team?	
What is your long-term strategy for the freelancers that you hire?	

What workspaces have you created for your blended team?	
What are your payment/ vending arrangements for your open talent?	
Are you leaving a door open for retiring employees to become freelancers?	
Can your managers adequately distinguish the different types of talent used?	

Also key to developing your future workforce strategy is understanding your company's industry ecosystem. Moreover, your company should be clear on the type of work that they are requesting to be completed. The relationship between firms' networks of stakeholders (suppliers, distributors, customers, competitors, government agencies) will vary according to the industry in which they operate, and as such, the self-evaluation questionnaire will help in determining the feasibility of and business case for increasing the use of open talent. However, first, there needs to be a clear understanding of the key differences between an employee and those who fall into the category of an independent contractor. If companies fear incorrectly labelling different groups of talent, they should always engage legal counsel or open talent platforms (E.g. Deel[26]) to ensure that they

---

26   https://www.deel.com/

are ticking the right boxes, especially if operating internationally. To help you along the journey, the below table provides some key differences between the two types of talent:

Employee	Independent Contractor
Work is largely defined by the employer	Free to determine their work and the way they work
Work is ongoing and may include a number of objectives/expectations as outlined in the job description and or contract.	Typically fills a specified knowledge gap and completes a specific project(s) for a defined amount of time.
Receives a fixed, determined salary (typically a monthly salary) and is subject to withholding of taxes, social security, etc.	Paid on a project-by-project basis or for a specific amount of time. It may vary based on project milestones. Contractors are typically responsible for their own taxes.
May receive tools and training to complete job	Does not typically receive equipment or training from employing clients.
Receives benefits such as social security, healthcare, sick days, pension and so on	Does not typically receive employee benefits such as social security, healthcare, sick days, pension and so on

The above differences reflect a general understanding and familiarity with the two categories of workers, but firms should always ensure that they research the legal definitions of these workers as there will be differences in their terms from country to country, or even state to state in some cases. So, what do these differences mean for managing a blended workforce? It means that companies must not only go back to the drawing board and adapt their internal policies and protocols, but they must do this with the knowledge of the parameters within which they operate, as well as a clear understanding of what they are trying to achieve. None of this is possible, however, without the right buy-in from key stakeholders. Our next section will further outline how companies can achieve this balance by developing the right blended protocols.

2. BLENDED PROTOCOLS: YOUR RULES OF THE ROAD

A firm's motivation for using freelancers should not be solely inspired by cost reduction. Beyond cost savings, freelancers can contribute significant strategic value and expertise to the organisation. However, an increase in blended work teams has implications for how HR manages their existing and future talent and forces people management to re-examine existing processes and establish new tools and rules for engagement. Blended work can become very chaotic as managers muddle through what type of relationship they should have with freelancers and what relationship freelancers should have with employees, if any. Organisations need a set of 'blended protocols' that act as a compass to direct engagement with atypical staff. With many retiring full-time employees now also choosing to continue working as independent contractors, organisations also have the chance to retain top talent if they create the right conditions for open talent. On top of that, the rise of freelancers provides organisations with a wider array of diverse talent, both internally and externally, in this increasingly blended workforce.

Setting Policies and Guidelines

When developing tools and guidelines to facilitate blended working, it's important to remember that there will never be a 'one size fits all' remedy for employers, given country-to-country differences in legislation. Rather, the key is to be aware not only of key regulations governing employment but also of the purpose and processes required to engage and smoothly integrate varying types of talent successfully. Following the cultural assessment highlighted in Chapter 1 will increase firms' confidence in bringing their future workforce strategy and blended protocols to fruition. Firms can further reduce their risk concerns by enlisting help from organisations dedicated to facilitating freelance hiring, most of which are applying innovative approaches to improving the accuracy of worker classification. For example, Deel is a company that provides an all-in-one platform where companies can automate the full management process for their globally dispersed workforce. This includes compliance and HR tools that cover processes like hiring, payroll, and mobility services. In recent times, they have also been working on developing the use of artificial intelligence based on case law, juries, regulations, and best practices across different jurisdictions to create an algorithm that will maximise the level of accuracy when classifying contractors and employees. We will speak more about platforms in the following section when deciding which platform to use. As more organisations take the bold move and venture towards increased open talent engagement, there will be increasing familiarity with the steps required and the support available to employers.

For a blended workforce to be effectively operationalised, firms must have the right underlying infrastructure and understanding of how they want to include independent workers. Also, Julie Turney, HR Expert and founder of HRatHeart stated that once a general approach to remote work is identified, it is essential to develop a decision-making framework to manage requests and mitigate compliance risks and articulate this through clear guidelines for approval. Companies should ensure that this process embeds a human component and not approach recruitment as a purely procurement or sourcing exercise. If businesses want to maintain an ongoing and valuable relationship with different talent stakeholders, then leaders must be deeply involved right from the beginning to ensure a personal touch and 'culture add.' Why is culture added and not fit? While companies want someone who can identify with their values, they seek freelancers because of their unique expertise and problem-solving skills and because they want to fill a knowledge gap in the organisation.

All companies should develop protocols and practices for their blended teams, and these should be clearly outlined and communicated to different types of talent. This should include a consistent programme around the organisation and engagement of independent contractors. This programme development required different firms to confront several questions around what different remote work scenarios might arise, who is eligible to work remotely, what approval and management guidelines should be in place, what compliance and risk management considerations were needed, and what benefits and employment terms were available for those working remotely. Julie believed that companies could reap significant rewards from such freelance engagement and relationships by mapping out these considerations and setting clear guidelines. By answering these key questions, they set the foundation for developing company policy guidelines for eligibility and compliance. The business should determine who the stakeholders are and what each of their roles and responsibilities are to create a strong governance structure with clearly assigned ownership. Assigning roles and responsibilities will allow the organisation to create a supporting process and the necessary tools to streamline this process. This will include steps from approving and documenting remote work approval processes to back-end operations such as payroll. The complexity of these supporting tools can range from simple guidelines and decision trees for internal use to technology tools that keep track of remote workers and the associated compliance obligations.

Legal risks around hiring and information sharing are always a major concern for companies. This could include compliance issues and loss of confidential information as a result of working with freelancers. With digital nomads, the location that they choose to work from may further complicate this, as local laws will dictate the nature of work. At the same time, many nomads in foreign countries operate off the grid, which exposes firms to further risks. To resolve this, organisations must develop mechanisms that can provide peace of mind to both the client and the worker in the absence of more reliable structures.

From Talent Acquisition to Talent Access: Identifying Organisational Needs:

To truly benefit from a more blended workforce, firms need to shift their thinking from talent acquisition to talent access. By doing this, they can create the right infrastructure to access a more diverse pool of talent that more aligns with their strategic objectives. This is only possible with more targeted interactions across departments to understand organisational needs. For example, key conversations should take place between HR, IT, and procurement teams to understand the evolving needs of the firm and ensure the goals of key stakeholders across the firm are aligned. To do this, a centralised database or platform where various departments can identify key priorities and challenges and input the skills required to address them is needed. This is no easy task and requires a dedicated person, ideally the designated leader of your blended workforce initiative, to orchestrate the effort. The pulling together of this data also makes departments and HR leaders more aware of common organisational challenge areas. Once this data is identified, it's next important to take inventory of the existing skill sets within the company's talent network. These skills should be stored within the same database and should be accessible across departments. HR platforms like

BambooHR, Factorial and HiBob are a few software options that allow HR leaders to identify existing employee skills, categorise these according to performance levels, and pinpoint internal skills gaps. These platforms can also be used to outline, categorise, and prioritise organisational projects that capture our company's key challenges. Moreover, platforms like Factorial allow companies to create a heatmap that highlights not only the skills possessed (e.g. JavaScript) but also colour codes these according to level and performance for future reference. Leaders can also choose to use more specialised open talent platforms that are designed specifically to source and manage freelancers. HR leaders must work closely with managers, collecting enough data to gain a more acute understanding of talent needs and determine the most appropriate method of acquiring specific skills and expertise needed. Once identified, these key stakeholders can determine if knowledge gaps need to be filled with a full-time employee role or whether using freelance talent could be more strategically beneficial. These actions should precede an attempt to engage freelance talent and even full-time talent.

Build Your Internal Talent Marketplace:

The term 'internal talent marketplace' was less used and relatively unfamiliar ten years ago. However, their creation and use are gaining momentum and have been made a priority by some of the world's most successful organisations (e.g. IBM, NASA, Unilever, Schneider Electric, Alibaba, Tencent, Google). Adapting Gloat's definition[27], an internal talent marketplace (ITM) refers to the use of internal job boards or innovative, AI-driven platforms to allow employees to seek new projects, gigs, job roles and other opportunities within their organisations. John Winsor identified the development of ITMs as one of the 3 key structures that underpinned an open talent

---

27   https://gloat.com/

Centre of Excellence (COE) with the goal of full organisational transformation.

Enhancing your ITM can deliver several benefits to companies, including better retention of full-time and younger talent, increased employee engagement, the reduction of departmental silos, better problem-solving, and enhanced flexibility across the company. In a context where individuals are seeking more fulfilling work experiences, ITM can help companies provide more interesting work opportunities that let the talent exercise a wider range of their skills, including their adjacent capabilities. Building these markets also gives internal talent the opportunity to build relationships right across the organisation as they work in cross-department teams on outlined projects. Companies can enhance their ITMs in several ways. Here are a few examples:

Posting internal projects/job opportunities:

- Forms can post unique company challenges on internal job or project boards and invite employees to choose what they want to work on. This not only enhances motivation and engagement but also results in more creative, multi-disciplinary solutions. It can also provide firms with more than one way to approach specific problems.

Horizontal Job Rotations

- Creating opportunities for employees to work across departments in completely different roles enhances solving unique challenges and can boost engagement in several ways. Not only will it reduce recruitment costs, but it will also provide talent with more interesting work, and hence, they will be less likely to look for external opportunities.

Coaching and Mentoring

- By providing developing talent with support and encouragement for their more experienced colleagues, individuals get the opportunity to identify growth areas in the firm and better understand how they can apply their range of skills across the organisation.

Third-Party Vendors

- Companies like Gigged.AI, Gloat, and Fuel50 now provide comprehensive ITMs for clients, including setting up the necessary platform, software and systems needed to post, monitor, and assess project outcomes. Through their platforms, companies have access to several HR applications and learning tools, as well as technical support to guide and develop leaders' and managers' user capabilities.

Building ITMs is now a must in firms seeking to expand, enhance innovation, and remain competitive, so companies must dedicate time and resources to its cultivation in a meaningful way. When done right, it will provide more creative work approaches and problem-solving, boost engagement and motivation, and help firms uncover and utilise a wider range of capabilities and skills. While this section looked at finding and matching internal talent with opportunities, the following section considers matching external talent with internal opportunities. Keep in mind, however, that neither process is mutually exclusive.

Open Talent: Deciding on Platforms

It is extremely important that, in a rapidly and constantly changing business environment, companies seek multiple independent opinions about how to solve an organisational challenge. When companies are exposed to several different solutions and can see where those opinions converge, they can have much more confidence in the final result and accrue the top results into a better-performing overall solution. To access a wider level of expertise, companies must embrace digital marketplaces and platforms as methods of sourcing globally dispersed talent who possess the knowledge needed to solve key organisational challenges. Then, they can begin to build a consistent internal process so that all stakeholders across different departments utilise the same platforms to ensure transparency and management. Moreover, for management who are new to the process, many of these platforms also help firms manage the freelance experience. Well-known and successful companies across the globe have already embraced the use of platforms to access more efficient ways to search, attract, employ, and engage independent workers. A part of creating this internally streamlined talent system is choosing the right open talent platform, and there are currently several great options in the marketplace. In the past, platforms like Upwork, Freelancer, and Fiver have provided such services but have been criticised for being more market-driven than personalised.

However, having responded to consumer feedback, these platforms have gotten better at tailoring their offerings to suit specific company talent requirements, combining the human touch with powerful, intuitive technologies like automation and artificial intelligence as key to attracting an increasing number of global freelancers. Companies like Talent Craft and HRCircle are also harnessing the power of technology to accurately match companies to their ideal freelance consultants in specific disciplines (E.g. IT and HRM).

There are several benefits of using freelance platforms. Some of these are listed below:

- More exposure to a wider range of freelance talent

- Quicker time to source and onboard talent.

- Can provide expert knowledge on managing freelance projects and talent.

- Adopts some of the company's risk in hiring freelance talent.

- Captures key data that helps the company understand talent needs and preferences.

While platforms aren't the only way to hire freelance talent (e.g., word-of-mouth referrals, third-party agencies), the above benefits can give firms greater confidence in engaging non-traditional talent. They increase the quality of talent available to companies by not only sourcing but also organising freelance talent into their specific disciplines. However, the platform industry is still relatively young, and hence, institutions have yet to develop and agree upon industry-wide standards.

Barry Matthews and colleagues at Open Assembly have developed a platform directory that allows potential users to input their criteria and choose the platform that is suitable for their needs. For example, clients can select based on the type of services they require and the type of relationship they want with freelancers (e.g. direct vs indirect). Companies can use the previously outlined questionnaires, and the data collected by the blended workforce (BW) strategy initiative to define the criteria that allow them to find the talent that they require to solve key challenges. Hence, when choosing a platform, HR leaders, in partnership with key stakeholders, must take several things into consideration, as not every platform is suited to the needs of all companies. Matthew Mattola of The Human Cloud developed a guide to help companies make this decision based on more closely examining what they are trying to achieve. In this guide, he recommends 3 key factors that companies should know:

1. The company's beachhead uses case and key departments to hire freelancers.

2. The primary region that freelancers will be hired from

3. The level of support needed when hiring freelancers.

As company stakeholders review their existing talent makeup and future needs, these factors encourage them to consider and determine the level of risk that they are willing to undertake. Depending on projected open talent requirements across the organisation, using a platform can offer firms greater indemnification through their network of partners, as well as a way to source and manage a higher quality of open talent. Currently, there are more than eight hundred platforms globally for companies to choose from, so firms must be clear about what they want to achieve from its use, whether the chosen platforms can satisfy future sourcing requirements if they provide enough global coverage, and the level of categorisations and specialisms offered. Other criteria that companies can use to select the right platform for them include enterprise maturity, the level of security, and compliance enhancements, but companies are not limited to only these.

Creating a Clear Job/Project Descriptions and Role:

One of the biggest impediments to the successful engagement of open talent or independent contractors is having unclear expectations and objectives from clients or companies, as well as loosely defined terms and conditions. In our 2020 research white paper, 'The Blended Workforce Revolution,'[28] we surveyed over two thousand

---

28   https://www.crowdpotential.co.uk/the-gighr-experts

independent workers and HR/business leaders from six regions to understand the challenges faced when the two parties work together. Freelancers complained that companies often failed to clearly articulate the objectives and scope of the assignment or project they were being contracted to fulfill, as well as how their role fits into the wider departmental or organisational mandate.

A key reason behind this was that when it comes to sourcing, organisations are used to creating and developing job descriptions rather than proposals when a specific skills gap or need for expertise arises. Many leaders still think about work and engaging talent as filling specific job positions and roles. However, industry leaders have observed that the people best fit to solve your company's problems are not sitting in your company.

Technology leader Justin Strharsky of Humyn.ai highlighted that our traditional model of working is built upon thinking about the kinds of skills they need and then trying to monopolise those skills for forty hours a week. The key drawback here, unfortunately, is that companies are met with Joy's Law[29], which posits that no matter who you are, the smartest people work for someone else (Bill Joy, Sun Microsystems). Therefore, existing recruitment approaches limit the skills that firms are able to attract based on geography and criteria around educational background and past experiences. However, thanks to technology, companies now have access to persons with less traditional skills and who go against the mould.

The work of Kareem Lekhani and colleagues at Harvard has shown that it's often people with adjacent skills (i.e. transferable skills) and not those with received wisdom or specialised within the specific career that can solve hard problems. Hence, HR leaders need to think differently about how they can engage the best expertise from

---

29   https://marchudson.net/academia/innovation-terminology/joys-law/

across the globe and deploy it effectively across their organisations. This requires firms to re-examine existing tools and practices used to hire, engage, and manage talent.

Many job descriptions are designed to include specific desired and required attributes and accesses according to specified educational background and level, as well as industrial experience. In reality, employees, once hired, typically do not use half of the skills outlined in the job description.

To engage the right talent as well as leverage employees' adjacent skills to solve organisational challenges, HR leaders and talent sources across the firms must get better at clearly outlining organisational challenges, breaking them down into specific tasks, and pinpointing the exact skills needed to solve them. The company's blended workforce initiative is the perfect testing ground for such experimentation, as designated blended workforce champions can pilot the development and use of task proposals for sourcing the most appropriate talent. This will inevitably lead to the identification of a wider range of skills across the organisational and the development of cross-functional teams.

Sourcing platforms like Fiverr, Upwork, and other platforms can provide companies with guidance on how to clearly define roles and tasks and create a well-articulated job or project proposals. Similarly, we've outlined below a few steps that companies can consider when developing job descriptions for hiring open talent and putting together blended workforce teams:

- **Evaluate the project's skills requirements:**

  - Break down the project into the individual tasks needed to complete the project successfully. Clearly articulate the scope of work and expected deliverables and determine whether internal or open talent is most appropriate.

- **Identify internal talent with the specified skills.**

  - Use the internal talent marketplace created by your BW initiative to identify employees with the necessary skills. Where teams are being created, surveys or interviews can be used to identify any further gaps in knowledge or capabilities.

- **Develop your clear job description:**

  - Provide a specific title for the job or project role and outline a summarised description of the tasks to be performed, the length of the contract, and the deliverables you hope to achieve. You can also include more company-specific details and even employ AI tools to help you further personalise your job description.

The above provides firms with a good point of reference as they begin crafting their new blended workforce journey. Through ongoing experimentation, they will continually review, refine, and optimise the process to serve better changing organisational demands. The below quadrant will explore how to create a positive work experience once the right talent is identified and hired.

3.   BUILDING THE WORK HABITAT

More and more companies are sticking with hybrid work models as more full-time employees continue to prefer increased flexibility, and others are choosing to leave their full-time positions altogether to work as independent contractors (sometimes with the very same firms). This trend alone actually removes barriers to a blended workforce as organisations move to more flexible working models, meaning it is easier to include a more blended workforce working in the same preferred way as many more permanent employees were, even as recently as 10 years ago.

With different types of talent demanding different work arrangements and levels of engagement, firms must make sure that they have varying and dynamic workspaces to facilitate their blended working arrangements. These spaces should create feelings of well-being and health and consider the specific flexible needs and, in some cases, health conditions of different workers. These health conditions include mental health, which has become a top priority in many organisations. Many knowledge workers, including HR professionals, experienced burnout post-pandemic and, as a result, abandoned their corporate lives to experience a more balanced work-life. Also, greater recognition of the needs of differently abled and neurodivergent talent has encouraged organisations to consider embracing not only increased flexibility but also different types of workspaces and environments that are more conducive to concentration and productivity.

As digital nomadism and remote work enter the mainstream, there are more reports of empty office buildings in major cities in the US as well as the UK and in parts of Asia.

Even with some companies issuing return-to-office mandates post-pandemic, office population levels have not returned to pre-pandemic numbers as more people opt for greater flexibility. Yet research has shown that employees still remain positive about returning to the office.

Despite this, a recent global study by Cisco has indicated that while some employees have no problem with returning to the office, more than half the respondents believed that their office spaces were not appropriate for hybrid working and wanted their office spaces to look and operate differently.[30] Transitioning towards a more hybrid model can deliver several benefits, including enhanced team communication, productivity, and work culture. If companies want to take advantage of these benefits, then they must start to re-imagine the office or work experience that they are offering.

Having read the above, your next question might be: what does a good hybrid work environment include? Firms should think of how they can fashion current workspaces that are more collaborative in nature and that inspire innovation. In many cases, a physical redesign of current office layouts was needed, along with increased technological infrastructure. The best way to know what redesign was most desired by your blended workforce was to ask them. Blended Workforce champions can consult with different groups of talent to understand what physical and or virtual environment they find most conducive to productivity and their own personal well-being. The information gathered, along with further data analytics around the impact of existing and future arrangements and the varying resources needed to achieve the redesign, would then be used by companies' Blended Workforce Initiative (BWI) to gain wider organisational buy-in and decide the next course of action. We've outlined some key factors for firms to consider in pursuing a hybrid redesign:

- **Ask:** Gather feedback from different groups of talent to understand their work needs. Ensure that feedback is collected across different generations and cultural settings (where applicable). Important in this will be to ask the independent workforce within your mix, and those in hybrid working arrangements as permanent or part-time employees, as to the best working habits and environments they may need help with at home…Not just in the office.

---

30 https://investor.cisco.com/news/news-details/2024/Cisco-Hybrid-Work-Study-Reveals-Companies-Need-to-Modernize-Offices/default.aspx

After all, one of the biggest lures of working remotely or nomadically is that it allows employees of any type to work in dynamic and unique environments. So, they need to be considered, too.

- **Analyse:** Use feedback and conduct further research and impact studies to determine the feasibility of the redesign and gain buy-in

- **Pilot:** Once support is gained, draft an initial redesign of a specified, designated area. Communicate intentions and secure volunteers to utilise and test the space. Agree upon a timeline for your pilot.

- **Review:** Gain feedback from pilot users, review and make revisions based on information collected.

- **Roll-out:** Based on the success of the pilot, begin to trial additional redesign in chosen designated spaces.

As organisations begin their redesign plans, they should give thought to seating arrangements, the layout of their current workspace, and any amenities that enhance workers' health and wellness. In doing this, they should do their utmost to ensure these spaces are eco-friendly and comply with sustainability goals where possible. A review of these might reveal that updates are needed to optimise the current work experience. Firms should also offer a mix of different workspaces, as working from home is not always an option for those who want to work remotely. Options might include co-working spaces, satellite offices, and work pods. HR leaders can also provide discounts or subsidies for private collaborative spaces or vouchers for public spaces like cafes. Firms should remember, however, that improving workspaces also includes enhancing the virtual work experience as discussed in previous sections and later in the book.

4. WORK EXECUTION

The work experience that you create for your people will determine whether you win the war for talent. This is why more and more companies are becoming preoccupied with creating the best work experience for their people. In a decentralised digital future, companies must craft a consistent, engaging, and satisfying work experience to suit a blend of freelancers, full-time employees, contractors, part-time employees, temporary workers, consultants, and other contingent workers. This begins at the sourcing stage, and the steps identified in the previous quadrant will help companies develop a streamlined process that creates a positive interaction with talent and achieves the desired organisational outcomes. A freelancer's introduction to the organisation begins at the sourcing stage. From there, individuals are already starting to make their judgement of the firm's culture and what their experience will be like during the project. In The Blended Workforce Revolution research white paper, more than half of the freelancers interviewed said that they probably wouldn't work again with clients who failed to provide the right climate and support during their interaction. Once firms are able to source the talent that they are after, a good onboarding process will give freelancers insight into what they can expect during the course of the project. However, firms need to begin thinking about this process differently, as there will be implications depending on the classification of the worker. Also, for a good work experience, both freelancers and internal talent must be onboarded into the newly created blended team. We explore these onboarding needs further in the following section.

Identifying the Desired Work Experience

When bringing freelancers onboard, companies often make either one of two opposing assumptions. The first is that their independent talent wants and desires the treatment and level of interaction as their in-house employees. Contrarily, the second assumption is that freelancers desire little to no contact with the firm apart from the communication required to complete the task. Either of these assumptions could be right or wrong depending on the individual freelancer. For that reason, it is important that organisations avoid treating independent talent as one homogenous group whose expectations and needs are the same. For example, our Blended Workforce white paper highlighted several different profiles of digital nomads (e.g.: retirees, travelling families, adventure travellers, Gen Zs on a gap year), which lent understanding to individuals' different expectations of company or client interaction. Underpinned by the legal parameters previously alluded to in this chapter, HR leaders must engage in open dialogue with freelancers to understand the type of work experience and engagement that would be acceptable and deliver satisfaction for both parties. Only from there can firms truly craft a work experience that is tailored to the needs of their different groups of talent.

It is also important to understand what managers and other in-house employees understand about and expect from their blended work experience, rather than waiting to see what work experience emerges. To do this, key stakeholders must get together and begin to map out the experience that they want. They can start this journey by asking themselves the following key questions:

1. Has the project objectives and roles been clearly defined for both your in-house employees and your freelancers?

2. What level of interaction is expected between different groups of talent?

3. Are the relevant access and resources available and in place to facilitate effective communication and teamwork?

4. What kind of challenges do you foresee, and have you thought of potential solutions?

5. What learnings and value can each group of talent contribute and take away from the experience?

The above represent a number of hurdles that companies typically run into when they stumble through the blended work experience. But with early consideration and effective preparation, all parties can reap the benefits of varying expertise in this diverse work experience.

Onboarding your Blended Work Team

Most freelancers engaged by organisations will never have any physical contact with the company that contracted them for the project, and this remote situation is often why freelancers are treated more casually once hired. As external service providers, freelancers won't possess knowledge of existing team relationships, interrelated objectives, reporting structures, or details of firm-specific challenges that may affect their assigned deliverables. Added to this, while being experts in their specified areas, they will have their own approach to work and way of doing things, which may cause friction with existing internal processes and negatively impact communications and interactions with full-time, in-house staff. Whether full-time or independent, remote or in-house, it's important that talent is given the right introduction into the firm and the necessary information and access to be able to fulfil their assigned role successfully. Developing an appropriate talent onboarding system allows companies to do this and exposes new starters to the organisational and team culture. Both full-time and independent staff must understand how their role fits into the wider team objectives and the overall organisational vision.

When different departments work in silos, they are often not aware of the existing and duplicated processes across the organisation. Hence, blended workforce champions (BWCs) should begin assessing what existing approaches to onboarding staff are already in use and whether freelancer onboarding arrangements, if any, differ from those applied to employees. As they do this, they should consult closely with their in-house legal and compliance teams or seek external legal consultation where these do not exist. If your company is already using open talent platforms, many of these already have simplified and systematic onboarding processes built into their service provision (E.g. Upwork, Worksome, YunoJuno), so companies should also explore these for suitability before duplicating their efforts. Whether you decide to use a platform onboarding process or create your own onboarding system from scratch, you want to create a process that is accessible, comprehensive, uncomplicated, personalised, and agile. Younger generations (e.g. Millennials, Gen Z) who are more used to instant access and seamless experiences will be less forgiving of onerous and time-consuming company processes.

How you onboard remote employees sets the tone for your employees' experiences down the road. Make sure to provide consistent and effective communication throughout the process because this will be their very first post-hire experience with the company. When creating your own BW onboarding experience (yes, experience!), you want to ensure that you have done the necessary preparation and research beforehand, as discussed in the previous paragraph. Following this, smooth and effective implementation and ongoing monitoring of the process once it's live is paramount. Below, we've outlined some key considerations to take board when designing your own system:

1. Gather and review necessary information around contractors of independent workers (e.g. classification, tax number, payment information, etc.) within the team to gauge the amount of organisational engagement permitted.

2. Have a suite of the necessary contracts and documents ready to be signed before commencing a working relationship. Based on the worker classification, these would typically include the appropriate work contract, data protection and confidentiality agreements. These documents should be developed, stored, and secured in the company's cloud database and ready to use when the sourcing process has gotten underway.

3. Initiate a one-on-one meeting (virtual or physical) where possible to welcome freelancers to the team and provide further clarity about the organisation, its reporting structure, key contacts, and project expectations. An interactive welcome video can also be pre-recorded and offered on-demand, with follow-up contact information for any freelancer questions.

4. Arrange a meeting to introduce freelancers to the project team members. During this meeting, team members can agree on communication frequency and channels, specific project deliveries and task timelines, and the nature of their working relationship.

5. Provide freelancers with any tools or information access that they might need to complete the project requirements successfully.

6. Monitor the onboarding process and collect feedback (e.g. surveys) to allow for continuous improvement. The feedback process should also include regular, agreed-upon check-ins with freelancers and other team members.

In developing their blended workforce onboarding process, firms should ensure that the timeline for completion is not overstretched and onerous. After all, many individuals choose the freelance lifestyle to escape bureaucracy and the corporate world and complete interesting work. While freelancers value good communication as it is necessary for achieving their project goals, not all freelancers want to be deeply included in regular organisational activities and interactions. The level of engagement desired by open talent can be discussed in the initial welcome meeting and subsequent team meeting. Different engagement work preferences point towards the need to create a truly inclusive organisation, with inclusion covering enhanced not only access, interaction, and opportunities but also a respect for different workstyles. We'll discuss this more in the next section.

An Inclusive Work Experience: Creating the right climate for truly awesome talent to shine.

Award-winning business leader Kaumudi Goda, who spoke with us about how to create more inclusive environments for open talent, shared that the mindful prioritisation of the principles of diversity, equity, inclusion, and belonging is critical to ensuring independent contractors are motivated, engaged, and high performing. She saw this as just as important for open talent as it is for full-time employees. So, how do we develop a future blended workforce strategy that serves as an enabler and not an impediment to the diversity and inclusion works the organisation is already doing? Here are her key recommended actions to take:

1. Prioritise high quality and personalised worker experience across the life cycle and across all categories of talent, whether gig, flexible or full-time.

2. Leverage technology as a tool for eliminating bias and amplifying and accelerating inclusion in recruitment and talent management.

3. Reframe the blended workforce impetus as an opportunity to further the diversity and inclusion agenda for the

organisation. In fact, it may be even easier to mindfully seek a diversity of qualified talent when hiring for project work.

4. Emphasise the importance of awareness and commitment to resolve equity issues. Listening and acting with courage and commitment when issues arise within the freelance and contract workforce will go a long way to making non-full-time workers feel included and cared for. In turn, this sense of belonging will enhance productivity, performance, innovation, and, thus, profitability.

In an inclusive work environment, all workers, no matter where or how they choose to work, feel a sense of belonging when engaging with the contracting firm. All team members identify with the purpose of the project and feel like a key part of the team, which creates the necessary underlying foundation for positive collaboration. Such inclusivity should translate in all areas, which means that freelancers should not be paid late but, like in-house employees, at the agreed time. Moreover, freelancers should have access to a project contact and project information when necessary.

OPENRULES ACTIONS ROADMAP TO GET YOU STARTED

Critical questions to answer during your 90-day implementation plan

Your template will help define the way forward. This can be curated in a workshop environment. Start by responding to the questions and adding your 90-day plans, actions, and measurables.

The OpenRules components	Questions to answer	Our ideas and 90-day plan action plan
Future Workforce Strategy	What are the current organisational reasons for using different types of talent? What language is being used to describe different groups of talent, and how does this affect organisational engagement? What are the current perceptions of using independent contractors vs. full-time employees? What are the future workforce needs of the organisation, and how can different types of talent be leveraged? How can DEI be enhanced across the organisation in future workforce planning?	

Blended Protocols	**Compliance:** What are the barriers to hiring and engaging different types of talent? **Legal:** What are the legal restrictions on the amount of time open talent spends engaging with clients? To what extent are companies permitted to define the nature of work execution by open talent? What are some key differences globally with regard to companies' ability to engage freelancers/open talent? What are the barriers to supporting/offering training and tools to open talent? **Ownership:** Who takes ownership of hiring, engaging, and the management of open talent? Where does the legal and compliance ownership sit—with procurement as owner or enactor? **HR Engagement:** What is HR's role in the engagement of freelancers?	

<table>
<tr>
<td>Blended Protocols</td>
<td>

How do we shift mentality across business and people leaders away from independent workers being 'managed services' to being a highly valued part of the workforce ecosphere?

What barriers or challenges exist to HR interaction with independent workers?

What support do managers need to manage a blended workforce?

Sourcing:
What are the company's existing talent streams and pipelines for independent workers and contractors vs. full-time employees?

What is the balance of push and pull between managers choosing talent sources vs. recruitment or procurement choosing approved channels?

</td>
<td></td>
</tr>
</table>

Work Experience	**Ownership:** Who is responsible for the experience of open talent during their engagement with the organisation? **Onboarding:** What are the current onboarding procedures for onboarding different types of staff? What are the onboarding needs for open talent vs. full-time talent? What legal restrictions exist to onboarding open talent? **Work Engagement:** What is the current experience of open talent vs full-time employees? **HR Support:** How might companies better adapt in-house practices to support open talent during engagement? To what extent do managers and full-time employees need support when engaging with open talent?	

| Work Habitat | **Workspace:**
Are there any dedicated workspaces.

What do productive and 'diverse-ready' work habitats look like in an office of the 2030s?

What spaces can be modified to provide the best environment for the rich diversity of employees who use the office? Including Neurodivergent mixed-ability employees?

How does your office habitat cater to independent workers who become valued members of your long-term workforce? (for example, to give them an option to work from an office)

What do the most effective home-based spaces look like?

What is our responsibility to provide guidance and budget to help our permanent, permanent, part-time hybrid workers optimise their home or other work setting?

What are the rules of the road for how people create remote or nomadic environments from which to work (for example, how they turn up for virtual meetings, in front of customers, etc.)? | |

| Work Habitat | **Workstyle:**
How do we accommodate different work styles while protecting internal productivity and ensuring that external customers experience high satisfaction?

How do we create a more flexible working style to recognise the rich diversity and generational mix of our workforce so that it is inclusive for all and exclusive for no one?

How do we measure working practices?

What are the qualitative and quantitative working practices and measures we need to adopt to track workforce satisfaction, productivity, effectiveness, collaboration, and communication?

How do we recognise new values and behaviours to support rapid culture evolution and building for an open workforce?

How are our new practices impacting the delivery of excellent customer experiences and longer-term customer journeys? | |

Chapter 5

OPENTOOLS:
THE SECOND ROOM

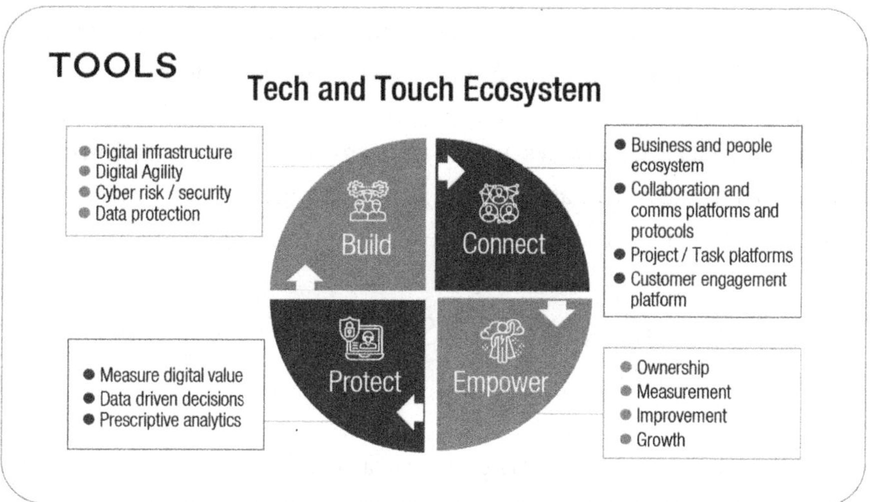

Figure 4: The OpenTools room

The aim of our 'Tools' room is to build an inclusive, data-protected, cyber-safe, trusted ecosystem binding together marketplaces, workplaces, the workforce (both permanent and independent employees, contractors, etc) and customers through enabling, empowering technologies and tools.

It is the seamless link between all elements that creates a true ecosystem rather than a series of individual platforms bound together by multiple Application Programming Interfaces (APIs). Also, APIs act as software intermediaries enabling communication between two applications. They provide a convenient means to extract and exchange data, facilitating accessibility both within and across organisations).

Therefore, our goal when considering the 'Tools' room is:

To seamlessly integrate enabling technologies with the human centre of the organisation, fuelling deeper and more meaningful collaboration, communication, empowered working and engagement across our people, whatever their designation, at all levels, everywhere, in a safe, secure way that can be measured from day one.

Getting this right allows us to manage our customer journeys better individually and as part of a broader marketplace of products, services, networks, and experiences.

THE OPENHR KEY QUESTIONS FOR THE 'TOOLS' ROOM

- How do we transform the organisation for the digital era while protecting and empowering our human resources (including permanent, part-time, and independent workers) and defending our high-trust customer relationships and other external partnerships?

- How do we become a cyber-safe, data-driven organisation that unleashes human potential at all levels through enabling technologies and tools, internally and externally?

5 important benefits of getting this right

- The customer, company and employees are hyper-connected through appropriate technologies and tools to power up the human touch.

- Empowered teams at all levels across the organisation can be unleashed to innovate, solve problems, and provide meaningful customer solutions collaboratively.

- Leaders and managers can be repurposed to focus more strategically on supporting individuals and empowering teams across the organisation.

- A digitally savvy organisation that is cyber secure and can move at speed through better data. Better data drives better decisions, which drive better performance across the organisation.

- The ability to measure the value deriving from digital and workforce transformation incrementally to the organic growth of the business. This will inform forward investments, decisions, and innovation plays to secure the long-term growth of the business as much as short-term health.

Watch out

Going for the 'fad or the fashion' rather than the 'function and form' where digital technologies and tools are concerned. We must go deeper to understand the most appropriate tech and tools relevant to our business and people that will enable greater automation of processes, empowerment of people, productivity (whether central or remote working), co-working, customer engagement, and results delivery.

The OpenHR challenge:

To create a new human resources framework relevant to a capable blended workforce and increasingly distributed workplaces, supported by appropriate tools and technologies.

Enabling and empowering the organisation to accelerate growth, resulting in a 21st-century business seamlessly and safely integrating the most appropriate digital technologies and tools with a stronger, more empowering human touch.

The OpenTools Room

Every business in the 21st century is operating in the midst of a huge acceleration of digital technologies that are impacting life, the workforce and the workplace. Businesses everywhere need to be more connected with a mobilised, engaged, and empowered workforce. With this in mind, OpenRules must be in place as the new human resources 'operating system' to underpin the attraction, management and retention of an increasingly blended and dispersed workforce. What comes after that is the glue to bind the component parts together – enter OpenTools.

According to a recent Boston Consulting Group survey of more than 5,000 managers and employees, over 80% said digital tools helped them get through the economic slowdown that the pandemic created[31]. Digital technology is the fuel that drives growth through more connected, collaborative, and agile human endeavour. We had to do it in the early 2020s, and we need to accelerate it as we look ahead to the 2030s.

---

31   https://www.bcg.com/publications/2020/
      the-evolving-state-of-digital-transformation

Therefore, at its heart, our OpenTools room is all about developing and managing a 'tech and touch' ecosystem fuelled by relevant and appropriate technologies that enable human productivity, engagement and performance in a way that is cyber-safe, protecting our business, our employees, our stakeholders, and our customers. In an era in which cyber risk and cyber-attacks are already costing economies and businesses trillions of dollars, it is imperative to build an ecosystem that is safe, secure, trusted, and workable: doing the intended job while having all the safeguards in place that are needed in the modern workplace.

Implementing your OpenTools approach begins with redesigning the technology. However, a consistent lesson is that it's not about technology alone. It's about technology, people and culture. Technology that enables but does not overwhelm, and technology that connects seamlessly across all functions and stakeholders without the need for binding sub-technologies.

For many organisations, the answer has become digitally enabled 'ecosystems.' According to Tata Consulting Services, this is defined as follows:

'A digital ecosystem is a network of stakeholders that connect online and interact digitally in ways that create value for all.'[32]

Digitally enabled ecosystems are leading organisations to enhance their own efforts by aligning with and connecting to partners, customers, and other external stakeholders – such as independent workers. The tools are appropriate technologies and tools that, more often than not, fuel communication, collaboration, and secure sharing at levels not as yet experienced. Digital ecosystems empower the workforce; they don't just support it.

---

32   https://perspectives.tcs.com/content/dam/tcs/pdf/perspectives/volume-12/Defining-Your-Digital-EcosystemThe-First-Step-in-a-Machine-First-Transformation.pdf

One of the most successful examples of an integrated ecosystem is provided by the Alibaba Group. Its businesses account for more than half of all e-commerce sales in China and reach more than two million merchants. Alibaba aims to become the world's fifth-largest economy. Jointly, Alibaba and Tencent currently have a valuation that is equivalent to the GDP of Switzerland. This is the corporate scale and size not witnessed in the c.20th Century and an increasing part of the landscape of the early c.21st Century when considering the likes of Amazon, Google, NVIDIA, Microsoft, and Alibaba.

Initially, the Alibaba ecosystem was simple – that is, it linked buyers and sellers of goods. As technology advanced, more business functions moved online internally, connecting with partners, suppliers, influencers, and shoppers externally.

Alibaba had Ant Financial for its initial online third-party payment platform (although that changed shortly after the failed IPO in 2021) and Alimama, an online marketing platform that provides sellers with marketing and advertising services. It has China Smart Logistics to provide real-time access to information that buyers and sellers use to improve delivery efficiency. It also has Aliyun, which offers platforms for cloud computing and data management. All of these technologies are interconnected and secure.

Leading organisations such as Alibaba continue to recognise new opportunities by using digital technologies to deliver greater customer experiences and value through a more connected internal effort that is enabled by appropriate technology that is bound together in a seamless ecosystem. Professor Mark Greeven, professor of innovation and strategy at IMD, calls this the 'ecosystem advantage.'[33]

---

33   https://hbr.org/2020/04/
       in-a-crisis-ecosystem-businesses-have-a-competitive-advantage

In order to get this right externally, we must first focus internally and follow the same sentiment. Safe, secure, appropriate, easy, and consistent communication, collaboration, data availability, and sharing are delivered through an enabling technology ecosystem, fuelling workforce productivity and performance. This should be the case when you are dealing with distributed workers, permanent employees, part of a growing independent workforce, partners, and other contributing stakeholders.

But how many business leaders and human resources professionals have the knowledge and skills to not only drive the strategy internally but also make it happen through seamless implementation throughout the business internally and externally? After all, this is where the data will come from to allow for faster decision-making, real-time data analytics and more. Perhaps for some, this overall represents a whole new skill set that needs to be developed. As soon as possible.

Digital adoption means proactively driving the use of appropriate digital tools to glue the organisation and its workforce together through ecosystems and being guided by ongoing data. Worryingly, there is a widening knowing-doing gap that exists within traditional HR in this respect, especially when considering the most senior human capital leaders in many organisations, who are more removed from the day-to-day. Recent research by the Digital Leadership Specialists (2024) reinforces this is an issue across functions and into the C-Suite:

'The majority of senior leaders researched across functions are becoming digitally detached from more operational leaders who are closer to ground level. Senior leaders are more confident about their organization's ability

to transform digitally, whereas leaders closer to the operational reality disagree with them. With reason.'[34]

There is a risk that senior leaders and HR professionals charged with planning and implementation around the OpenTools room do not have the knowledge or know-how to execute the strategy successfully. This is an all-level journey, and the OpenTools room provides the most important elements to learn and implement.

Therefore, the OpenTools tech and touch ecosystem becomes an accelerator for the organisation's transformation and as a measure of the ongoing value of its digital and workforce changes. It is important when considering your tech and touch ecosystem to build in measures from day one. Why? Because change will be ongoing and evolutionary, and having data from the get-go to allow for more fluid decision-making, problem-solving, opportunity assessment, and more will be key.

To reinforce this, the Digital Leadership Specialists cite Aeroflot's digital transformation as being the fundamental success factor in moving from being one of the worst airlines to one of the best:

'Aeroflot has transformed itself from one of the worst to one of the best airlines. It turned to digital technology to improve its operations, report passenger bookings and schedule customer care. Specifically, it created dashboards that provided management with an instant overview of more than 450 key performance indicators. It measured its ongoing transformation from the start, and this helped it steer implementation success. The company also aggregates information from sensors installed on the plane. This facilitates visibility into aircraft performance and preventive maintenance, resulting in reduced costs.

---

34   https://performanceworks.global/digital-leadership-specialists/

'In executing any strategy, identifying and tracking the right measures is one of the toughest challenges. Adopting digital, creating digital and human ecosystems, measuring digital value, and being driven by real-time data have become even tougher because many areas are new. But it is critically important. Therefore, once you have the right scorecard relevant to your business, employee, and customer needs, it will act as your lighthouse to guide the organisation through the difficult path ahead.'

Open Assembly understands the importance of open talent models supported by binding digital ecosystems. We talked to its CEO, Barry Matthews, to find out more:

INTERVIEW WITH BARRY MATTHEWS, OPEN ASSEMBLY

To illustrate OpenTools in action, we spoke with Barry Matthew, CEO of Open Assembly, who outlined how his team helped UST Global create the infrastructure for an award-winning open talent model. Barry is a talent trend-spotter and human cloud pioneer with a record of success in blended workforce enablement. In 2021, he merged Open Assembly with Re-source, a consulting firm that helped enterprise clients tap into the open economy. Currently, he works with senior executives on talent strategy and co-hosts the podcast 'How the Future Works.' The following interview is from our conversation with Barry:

Jeremy Blain and Dr Rochelle Haynes: Please tell us a bit about the background infrastructure that was needed to support the tech system.

Barry Matthews: Our consultants work with business leaders to develop new and dynamic approaches to workforce planning. That allows them to add capability, create scale without adding headcount, and move cost from fixed to variable. So, we wrote a case study based on our work with UST Global (a provider of digital transformation solutions and services), and I'll share what we've been doing with them. We followed five key steps to build our open talent ecosystem: assess, learn, experiment, build and scale. We are involved in critical business functions. We identified challenges and solutions. We started small experiments, learned lessons, and prepared for scale. And you know, these were just examples. This required some initial strategy work to assess the viability of it, you know. We evaluated external and internal marketplaces to determine the fit. We reviewed virtual desktop interface solutions because security has always been a huge concern. Then, we carried out pilots with different teams to experiment to see what works and what doesn't. Then, we have evolved the number of platforms that provide services into use, so they're now operating as part of an ecosystem. So, I basically then wrote some texts, and I started actually with the final stage, which is the transformation stage.

Jeremy Blain and Dr Rochelle Haynes: That sounds really intriguing. Can you tell us a bit more about how this ecosystem works in UST Global?

Barry Matthews: What we've done at UST is transform how they fundamentally access external skills. So, they now take this flex-first approach. Previously, they just used to look at traditional things, and we need to hire people first. Now, the hiring managers use the centre of excellence daily…a physical centre that we'd set up. And we have someone who runs that centre. It also supports several functions that Open Assembly supports. So, when demand for talent comes into UST Global from their account teams, it goes to a workforce management function. And that workforce management function optimises this. Companies need to think about the deployment of talent cloud models. So, how do you use digital platforms to supplement, augment, or get expertise?

We believe that the second big area is open innovation platforms. So, using an open mindset and a crowd-sourced mentality methodology to bring in new ideas to your organisation to deliver innovation, and we think the crowd, in a curated way, plays a really important role in bringing new ideas to play.

Jeremy Blain and Dr Rochelle Haynes: So how does that work in practice?

Barry Matthews: Our logic is that we can provide all of that in one place. So, let's assume UST says, 'Okay, well, I've got a work request. Yeah, I need a freelancer who's got Microsoft as your DevOps skills. I need them for 60 days, and I've got $300 A Day to spend. They need to be somewhere in the US, but they can work remotely. The start date's next year, and the approver is so, so we've confirmed Johnson and Johnson's clients. Do I need a VDI? Yes. So, all of that is in one form. Because you need to act, you need all of that information, right? If you try to work with a freelancer, all those things need to be in place. Doing that without a technology platform or some form of ecosystem would be challenging. So that's the first thing is you have a request. And that's got to be collected digitally somewhere.

The second thing is, once you've got that request, which is important from an enterprise perspective, you ensure you have actually validated that they are serious and have signed. Otherwise, you will waste so much time. Right?

So, we're going to make sure that that's completely validated, which is where we use a Red, Amber, and Green RAG system.

The next thing we are able to do is broadcast that requirement to a number of different sources. And that can be talent platforms, like the ones that are basically Braintrust, talk GTI, TopTal, Upwork, Freelancer.com, whoever, right? Or it could be, you know, in this case, Kelly or Worksome, or it could be individual freelancers who've registered on USGS talent cloud, or it could be leavers or alumni. And in the new system that we will have, as we post that work request, it will appear as a request that these guys who are part of our system can see. So, it's like an exchange. So, it's almost like our own talent lab and freelance talent platforms, right? So, we put the job out, all of the members of our ecosystem can see it proactively, and then we'd have to push it to them. They get an alert and can then respond and submit candidates. So, without that technology, this process is all manual and incredibly difficult to do from lots of different sources.

So then, that third bit is once they've submitted the perfect candidates to our system, we're able to review them then, filter them, then go from 20 candidates to the top five UST teammates, then only one through. We just want the best freelancer. It might be from Kelly Services or Upwork. We don't care as long as the freelancer can meet the requirements of number one.

Therefore, we can more easily facilitate the review and interview processes. Are they still available? Do they want to work? Is it the right price? We have all the data, and the decision can be informed, quick and easy.

Jeremy Blain and Dr Rochelle Haynes: Is that where you partner with CXC Global? Could CXC Global address the compliance side of it?

Barry Matthews: Exactly. And what we're trying to do now, and we haven't done yet. We are trying to integrate different partners into our cloud so that we can do this digitally. We're providing CXC with details. They go off and classify, (i.e. make sure that 'John Smith' can work in the UK, within IR35, or in India, whether we're in California or wherever). So, it's a bit of a detailed process, but it's still super important that all of that is done. Then when at UST, for example, access to relevant cloud systems for a freelancer to add maximum value is crucial. Because if the piece of work is just 60 days, then you don't want to be shipping a laptop to the other side of the world or wherever it might be.

In short, getting access to systems in a secure way is crucial, and we are exploring methods of integrating this, so you get systems access in a controlled way really quickly. Then, we make sure the freelancer signs relevant documentation, such as GDPR or data confidentiality, having all of that in a system that captures it, stores it and offers traceability.

It's good for us so we can make sure we've got everything collected and there's data on everything, and without any form of platform this would be very difficult to manage. Then, once all stakeholders have signed that off the work can start, our freelancer can commence work, where needed, and put in their weekly timesheets, their status reports, and whatever has been asked for in the statement of work.

If something goes wrong, they or the client can escalate it to us, and we can help solve any challenges or issues.

The freelancer completes the piece of work, and they then get paid. How? We pay the source, and it might be Braintrust, Kelly Services, or Worksome, and then they pay the freelancer. From there, we invoice UST Global, UST pays us, and UST may also pay a fixed monthly fee to organise the service.

Once the freelancer has finished work for UST Global, they are automatically put into the talent cloud so that they can be deployed again very quickly. For example, if UST Global wants them back, they can be accessed very quickly again, and partners like Braintrust, Freelancer etc will get their commission.

That said, the essence of our service is having access to the right people at the right time in the cloud. Everything a potential client needs is there, and they could do a real-time search, within specific parameters. For example, 'I'm looking for Microsoft Accredited DevOps specialist.' From the system, we can see Joan Smith, and she has five stars. We can also see their work record with us, all background checks, and their compliance status as an independent contractor. they've already got background checks. It's so incredibly efficient.

It's good for the agencies and the platforms like Freelancer because they're getting good repeat business. And we facilitate the whole thing. It is an end to end, binding ecosystem linking independent talent, through their preferred platform of choice (i.e. Upwork) to specific and targeted client needs, with all the checks and balances completed. It's fast, safe, efficient and effective.

Jeremy Blain and Dr Rochelle Haynes: That sounds brilliant, and it is exactly what is needed to digitalise, track, and measure ROI on the open talent work process.

Barry Matthews: Yes, and there are a number of similar marketplaces like PWC's Talent Exchange. It's for direct sourcing, mainly in the US. So, for any talented independent worker they can browse PWC roles, find out about them, and more.

When you have a look at Talent Exchange, you'll see candidates with skills in specific areas of need and the whole thing becomes a more efficient direct sourcing platform. areas. So, it's basically a direct sourcing platform.

What we're offering at Open Assembly is something similar to this, but across platforms, agencies, regions, countries and multiple Talent profiles. It's everything combined into one as a one stop independent talent resource hub.

It's my view that every company, of whatever size, should have a talent platform strategy. I think that the obvious benefits of talent platforms using digital technology to link supply and demand have remained unfulfilled. We've been saying for 20 years how digital technology will enable us to link supply and demand and it hasn't really happened yet en masse. But it is still a $14 billion market, and it grew at 29% last year. So, it's growing at an accelerated rate.

Jeremy Blain and Dr Rochelle Haynes: Definitely, and I believe it will continue to grow. So, what tech tools and skills do people management professionals need to utilise such an ecosystem to benefit companies efficiently? What skills should HR professionals be trying to prioritise?

Barry Matthews: I think all HR professionals should be learning about generative AI, right? I mean, if ever there was a technology that's going to change the way HR works, it's generative AI, in my opinion, because sourcing, effectively HR, is really looking after the recruitment process, being able to support the matching of demand with the right supply, whether it's freelance or full-time or whatever.

That plays into the hands of data, and the entire application tracking system can, therefore, be automated and supported my tailored Generative AI to access real-time data and inform decisions at speed. So, I think every HR professional will have some AI co-workers fairly soon. It is so important for HR leaders and experts to get to grips with digital transformation and evolving technology options available. It's about automating everything, cloudifying everything and underpinning all activity with robust data, managed by your tailored AI. It still surprises me just how manual the process still is in many organisations, and HR professionals need to embrace a steeper learning curve if they are to be the champions of all talent for a digital world.

If I were to advise modern HR professionals, I would also help them understand how Web3 and the Blockchain can help them get things done. Securely, safely and with cyber traceability. So Generative AI and Blockchain are 'now' gamechangers for the most enlightened HR leaders and professionals out there.

Jeremy Blain and Dr Rochelle Haynes: I'd absolutely agree with that one. What do you think would be the biggest digital challenges faced when trying to develop and use this ecosystem work?

Barry Matthews: The fact that enterprises all work inside silos. So, at the moment, there will be a team in 'company A,' let's say, who work with the contingent workforce, and they'll be another one who works with outsourcers. Then there will be a third and they're looking at multiple different talent platforms. All these three things, in most cases, will be treated separately, rather than as a potential joined-up ecosystem. Mainly due to the complexities within traditional company structures. For example, siloed thinking, departments not talking to or sharing with each other, etc.

To break that chain, if you could get your data integrated and searchable across the organisation, then that would be incredibly helpful. Using consistent language, talent terminology and more. That can also get in the way for sure.

One other element critical to all this working is the deep understanding of legislation across the world in regard to freelance and independent talent recruitment and use. For example, if they are working from outside that region, into the region, are there specific rules that the European Union may have in place; and how different might that be to US or China rules for the same. It can get complicated but it's a central accelerator of success.

Jeremy Blain and Dr Rochelle Haynes: So, looking at the measurements, trying to make sure you're getting what you want from this ecosystem and from your digital and distributed workforce, what do you think should be included in a company's digital scorecard?

Barry Matthews: I think that a couple of areas should be prioritised. So, I have demand, and I'm looking for supply. How long does it take me to go from creating the work request and the demand to actually finding somebody and getting them to start work?

That time should be measured as a KPI from day 1.

The second measurement, I think, should be around cost. I'd have a keen eye on the cost of talent acquisition. So, understanding the cost of my various freelance recruitment or management activities; who else needs to be involved; what measures should be in place and how do we track it all in real time?

This will help reduce the cost of acquisition as much as is possible. So, a crucial element to master. Which is all part of the broader measurement of cost, productivity, speed of action and results.

Simply put, if I have ten people in my team, five internal and five external, then I'd want to measure the total cost of my workforce; compare relative costs and outputs, and that should link to productivity measures. All this gives me the data to make decisions - whether that is around skills building, coaching, reward, recognition, performance management or, crucially, the day-to-day optimisation of my workforce.

OPENTOOLS QUADRANT BY QUADRANT

In order to help other organisations replicate the success of companies like Alibaba and Open Assembly, we created the OpenTools room and anchored it around the four key components that lead to success according to organisations who are embracing open talent and an OpenHR approach.

Our OpenTools insights come from case examples we have already discussed in this book, brand new research, our own working practices with small, medium, and large clients internationally, and interviews which have provided us with the best practices being adopted by forward-thinking organisations, the C-Suite and human capital leaders.

Each of the four components of the OpenTools room is reliant on and closely connected to the others, providing a step-by-step approach to adopting digital through an ecosystem-centred approach that is safe, secure and easy to use.

Quadrant 1: Build

Aim: To create an ecosystem to support internal and external working, collaboration, communication and service delivery – appropriate for both permanent and independent workers and other stakeholders critical to business success.

This starts with a connected digital infrastructure fuelled by appropriate technologies that accelerate collaboration, communication and action across the business. It becomes a catalyst and a platform for agile working.

It is grounded in security and safety protocols to protect data, people, business, and intellectual property. This is of critical importance. In fact, according to a critical BitSight study conducted by Forrest Consulting, 38% of companies reported business losses due to hacking concerns.[35]

Having a robust cyber strategy is central to employee, shareholder, stakeholder, and customer confidence in your business, as well as your ability to manage digital challenges like cyber-attacks, hacks and data loss. With it, you have a strong foundation. Without it, you risk loss of business and loss of credibility as a business.

The first, therefore, is to analyse where you are now, where you need to be and how to get there as a cyber roadmap.

Quadrant 2: Connect

Aim: To mobilise and engage stakeholders internally and externally through appropriate technologies that connect and drive collaboration and ease of communication for teams, groups, project working and customer interaction.

Building an ecosystem that enables and underpins how people work together, communicate, and collaborate is a major preoccupation of the modern workplace. Especially when we consider that traditional ways of working are evolving and we have distributed teams, increased numbers of independent workers, dispersed office locations and more.

---

35 https://www.cnbc.com/2019/09/03/half-of-hacked-companies-say-they-struggle-to-attract-new-customers.html

For many, this is the opportunity to reinvent how the organisation is structured and how human resources is better supported for the OpenHR era.

This may represent a culture shift for some and will redefine the way things are done across the organisation. It is critical that everyone is on board and modelling the new way and new behaviours and recognising others for doing so. Equipping them with the tools, the tech, and the know-how to enable their work while not overwhelming will be a key success factor to measure from day 1.

The article *'Collaborative technology: definition, benefits and features,'* from the team at indeed.com articulates the need clearly.

'The modern workplace often involves collaboration. Technological innovations can enhance cooperation and solve challenges associated with regular physical meetings, long distances between collaboration members and prolonged periods of collaboration. Incorporating these innovations may be convenient for the users and can improve efficiency in the workplace.'[36]

When done correctly, people have the tools they need, the know-how they require and an understanding of the way we all need to work together, wherever we are located and whatever our designation. The new ecosystem powers project teams and task management; it enables more efficient and speedy customer interaction and helps to accelerate

---

36   https://uk.indeed.com/career-advice/career-development/
collaborative-technology

decision-making horizontally within empowered teams and vertically through to strategic decision-making in the boardroom.

Quadrant 3: Empower

Aim: A digital ecosystem enabling the organisation and associated stakeholders to be truly empowered, leading at their level and taking ownership of actions and projects that may well be additional to their core job role.

This more empowering way of working is being adopted by many organisations – whether small, medium, or large. They are experiencing how a truly empowered workforce can contribute to the business, improve their roles as part of other projects teams and groups and, ultimately, grow the overall skills bench of the organisation. That, in turn, leads to a positive impact on quantitative business measures: the bottom line!

Therefore, implementing the most appropriate technologies, tools, and processes accelerates everyone's ability to contribute more and be more engaged in the overall health of the business. It is motivating and attractive and supports macro measures such as employer branding, attraction of talent, retention numbers and employee satisfaction.

In fact, a recent article from CMSWire found that 54% of business leaders plan to invest more in user-friendly collaborative solutions[37]. It is as simple as that: appropriate technology that fuels greater empowerment and collaboration and focuses on what matters. The technology should be largely invisible, allowing the human touch to come to the fore.

---

37   https://www.cmswire.com/customer-experience/
      dear-business-leaders-stop-treating-people-as-data/

ChiefExecutive.net goes a step further and highlights three ways to truly empower employees through an appropriate technology strategy, adding that any digital tools and tech should support employees and not overwhelm them with process and systems fatigue:

1. Consolidate and simplify your approach.

2. Use artificial intelligence to automate

3. Preach digital accountability to your team

In his book '*Unleash the Inner CEO - Make Distributed Leadership a Reality*,'[38] Jeremy Blain makes a case for empowered working being central to competitive advantage in the transformed, digital-human, modern workplace:

'The fast pace of how we live and work today is driving incremental and radical change in business and is becoming the new normal. Some organisations are coping with this fast-paced change, but many are left behind. The rate of change is catching companies unaware across the globe. Transforming organisations to prepare them for the future is no longer a question of when and whether it's a good idea but has become an urgent matter of how to transform.

As a result, many are crying out for a new business model to help them successfully transform at both digital and human levels and propel their organisations into a prosperous and exciting future. Such a model must drive more diverse, distributed, and collaborative leadership by unleashing the power of people, which is enabled by appropriate technologies, flatter structures, and repurposed line management. The age of empowerment is upon us, and those enlightened organisations committed to making it a reality are the

---

38   https://amzn.eu/d/j5qzvYD

very ones winning in marketplaces everywhere. From a customer standpoint and with their employees.'[39]

In his book, Jeremy Blain provides the knowledge and toolkit for how to build an empowered workforce in two ways:

- Firstly, creating the conditions at the organisational level will allow leaders at all levels to flourish without fear and with the support of the executive leadership and coaching-centred line managers.

- Secondly, it provides a well-planned 90-day road map for individuals at all levels who commit to the journey. This can be further supplemented by a personal development parallel track and a unique self-assessment that finally provides a platform to develop the behaviours, skills and knowledge required to be a successful leader, regardless of level, job description or functional role.

Quadrant 4: Protect

Aim: To clarify the 2 ways to focus on organisational protection behind a digital ecosystem for customers and employees.

i) Protecting business health through faster, better, data-driven decision-making at strategic and operational levels.

ii) Managing cyber risk, data protection and digital challenges in a way that defends the organisation, its people, stakeholders, customers, independent workers and partners from the increasing risk – and cost – of hacking, data breaches and cyber-crime.

---

39   https://performanceworks.global/theinnerceo/

If your 'Build' component within OpenTools can be referred to as the 'new world,' then your 'Protect' component will act as your guiding light to help you get there. It ensures your transformation is going in the right direction and helps you to take corrective action when necessary. In essence, this means creating a digital scorecard that will enable you to demonstrate the value of the transformation you are leading (for your OpenHR framework as much as this OpenTools room).

Because Implementing OpenHR is a new initiative for many organisations, the current scorecard and ways of measuring return on investment and experience are typically not 'fit for purpose.' A new approach requires new measures. This is particularly true when creating a human resources framework that may not have existed before and will be delivered through an integrated digital ecosystem, which enables the human resources, inside and outside of the organisation, to new, improved levels. According to Boston Consulting Group (BCG), this is of critical importance: 'Digital measures rewire organisations to perform better — not through a one-time change but through a fundamental reboot of how work gets done.'

It is also critical that leaders and managers across the business take time to ensure the new scorecard is driving the right actions throughout the organisation. It means ensuring everyone is intimate with the OpenHR strategy, its operational objectives, and the overall new measures used to track progress and impact the business.

When the right measures have been selected, people in each area of the business will know what is expected of them as they integrate new ways of working with enabling technologies and tools. This then allows them to effectively align and coordinate initiatives across functions and with their customers. This is precisely how our OpenTools approach accelerates measurable empowerment, collaboration, and more efficient communication through appropriate, connected, and enabling digital threads that benefit individuals, teams, and the organisation.

When organisations don't upgrade their measures behind new transformations, they won't know where they are along their journey and in which direction to head. This is at the heart of our OpenTools 'Protect' component. By keeping the direction true and tracking progress as a constant, organisations can avoid common pitfalls that result in slower progress or, worse, failure.

The second part of our 'Protect' quadrant links closely to where we started – building the new digital infrastructures behind safe and secure protocols, with cyber security and data trust at the top of our minds.

To protect the business through the OpenHR transformation as a whole, we must not only measure digital value but also measure and enhance our cyber security protocols and data management efficiency. We must be prepared to build on where we started as new threats emerge to challenge our newly developed digitalised ecosystem, and we must ensure that dedicated resources are allocated to monitoring, managing, and feeding back at the leadership level as a constant.

The following questions and template will help you and your organisation or team get into the details. The questions that must be answered are developed from the success being enjoyed by best-in-class companies of all sizes around the world.

OPENTOOLS ACTIONS ROADMAP TO GET YOU STARTED.

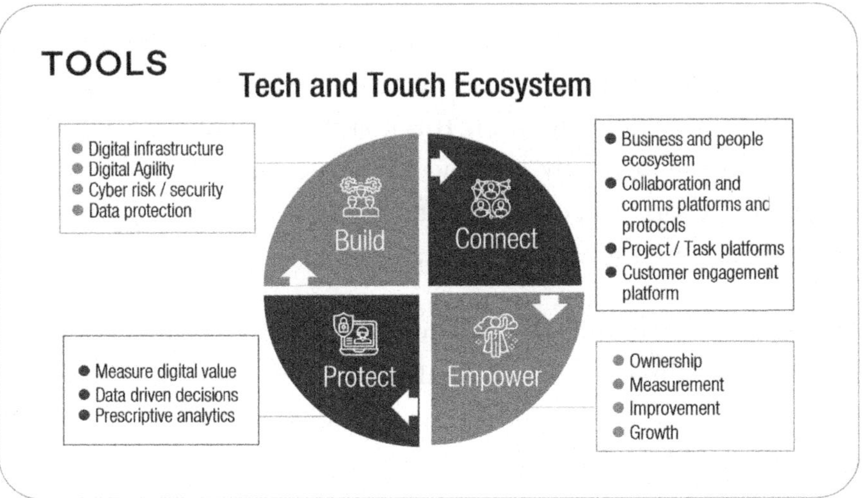

Critical questions to answer driving your 90-day implementation plan.

	Questions to answer	Ideas and 90-day plan action plan
Build Digital infrastructure Digital agility Cyber risk and security Data protection	What does our digital ecosystem need to deliver? • Internally • With our blended workforce and other external partners • With our customers What futureproofing/ upgradability are we building to ensure ongoing systems evolution and undisturbed agile working?	

Build	How does this inform our cyber strategy, planning, execution, and ongoing monitoring?	
Digital infrastructure	What existing technology can we build on, and there are new opportunities?	
Digital agility	How quickly do we need to make progress?	
Cyber risk and security	How do we know we are making the right decisions, and what measures accompany the journey?	
Data protection	How do we get started, and who will lead and manage the plan?	
	What are the new internal processes whereby any cyber risk, hack or security issue/breach can be escalated to HR and IT within seconds of it being identified or suspected?	
	What protection, safety and security measures need to be built in from day 1?	
	What is our organisational and workforce exposure to cyber risk now and within the next two years?	

Build	How do we enable agile working through appropriate digital technology and tools while protecting the security of our business and the personal safety of our people (whether permanent workers, employed independent resources or other value-adding stakeholders)?	
Digital infrastructure Digital agility Cyber risk and security Data protection		
Connect Business and people ecosystem Collaboration and communication platform and protocols Project / Task platforms Customer engagement platforms	How does our digital ecosystem enable and support our blended workforce? How do we use the digital ecosystem and tools therein to connect and bring people together in ways that boost productivity, collaboration, communication, and our collective performance? What technologies and tools are the most appropriate to streamline our internal business collaboration and communication? How does our digital ecosystem allow for winning collaboration and secure collaboration and trading with our customers?	

Connect Business and people ecosystem Collaboration and communication platform and protocols Project / Task platforms Customer engagement platforms	How will our technology ecosystem support greater empowerment of our people and broader, self-owned project management and delivery? What do we need to do to ensure everyone, internally and externally, uses the tools appropriately and with cyber risk and data protection in mind? What training and on-the-job coaching needs to be in place from day one? • The technology and tools upskilling • What human skills are associated with best practice communication, collaboration, and productive co-working (remote and face-to-face)? How does our technology secure ongoing feedback and new ideas from our internal teams, external stakeholders and customers to ensure we are embracing agile working and constantly evolving?	

| Empower

Ownership

Measurement

Improvement

Growth | What does leadership at all levels look like for our organisation?

What new workforce structure/processes are needed to underpin a new age of empowered working internally and with our partners and customers?

What management and budgetary protocols are in place to support innovation labs, new ideas, trials and projects?

How do we convince our people that we are building an empowering culture and will follow up words with actions?

How do we provide our people with the tools and the training for them to truly take ownership of tasks and activities beyond their job description?

Who leads the initiative at the board and HR senior level to bring in the structures and rules that become the foundation for unleashing leaders at all levels?

What are the qualitative and quantitative measures we need to track the impact on people, the business, and our customers? | |

Empower Ownership Measurement Improvement Growth	What improvements are we looking for across our permanent and independent workforce, as well as external partners? How do we support that with the training, the correct measures, and the appropriate reward infrastructure? How do we measure individual improvement? How does a 'growth mindset' underpin our approach alongside the appropriate technology, tools and skills building?	
Protect Measure digital value Data-driven decisions Prescriptive analytics Risk management and ongoing security	How do we measure overall digital value derived from our workforce transformation and digital ecosystem? How will we be able to demonstrate the success of building our digital/human ecosystem? What does an efficient data-driven organisation look like? How do we use AI to deep dive into our data to inform, advise, accelerate and enable our business?	

Protect	How do we upskill everyone to use better data visualisation techniques to support our new agile working?	
Measure digital value		
Data-driven	How has employee and independent worker satisfaction improved since implementing our plans?	
decisions		
Prescriptive analytics	How has customer service and satisfaction improved through more efficient working internally and externally?	
Risk management and ongoing security		
	By leveraging our predictive analytics, what needs to be done today to manage for tomorrow?	
	How can the data we use prescribe our ongoing actions and feed into forward business strategy?	
	How can we build safety and security protocols to pick up new digital threats to our business and our people and have a 'ready to go' contingency plan in place to implement?	

Chapter 6

OPENSKILLS: THE THIRD ROOM

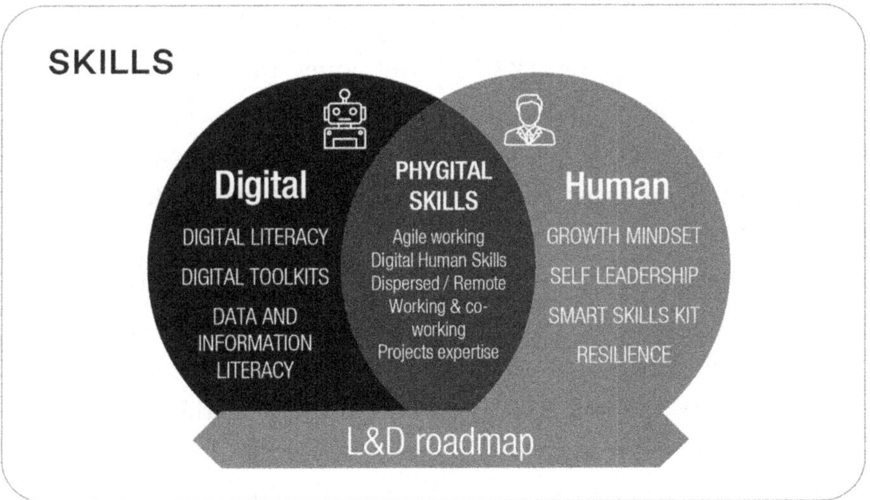

Figure 5: The OpenSkills Room

Organisations must think 'evolution' and not revolution. The creation of a blended workforce will not be seamless, and it will not happen overnight. Sometimes it's important to slow down first for us to accelerate on a more solid base. It will require several internal changes, not only physical and technological developments but also a mindset shift that starts from the very top of the organisation.

Resistance to the change is inevitable, as in-house employees will feel threatened by the proposed shifts. Organisations often neglect the human component by not considering the capability and readiness of their workforce to make this shift. Many workers fear that the introduction of new technology coupled with the procurement of independent talent will not only make their jobs more difficult but even possibly redundant. Others might fear the cultural shift will upset their status quo and that they won't be able to keep up with new job demands.

The third room, OpenSkills, addresses the knowledge gap that is inevitably created with the wide-scale shift towards digital adoption and embracing more agile and independent talent. Research has shown that two out of every three companies undertaking a journey of digital transformation fail in their attempts to introduce and embed meaningful change[40]. Hence, in addition to introducing the right technology, firms must also reflect on how they can prepare their people to confidently and rapidly adapt to the ever-changing world of work. A key part of this is empowering and equipping them to work with globally dispersed and independent stakeholders. The World Economic Forum stated that fifty per cent of the workforce will need to be re-skilled by 2025 if they are to adapt to the continuously changing work environment. Organisations must support employees in learning to work differently and capitalise on their transferable skills to remain relevant and adapt to the ongoing change that has now become the norm in our business environment and wider society. With this in mind, the need for a new human resources management framework and the role of HR professionals in developing a learning and development roadmap that executes these mandates has never been more important.

---

40   https://performanceworks.global/digital-leadership-specialists/

Goal:

To create a continuous culture of learning and adaptation where organisational members are capable of easily adopting digital and can transition into new roles when necessary. To help leaders and talent alike leverage all of their skills to solve key organisational and societal challenges

The OpenHR Key Questions when considering OpenSkills:

In this chapter, we mainly answer the following questions:

1. What skills and capabilities do organisations today need to engage different types of talent better?

2. How do we prepare and equip our workforce to be more autonomous, future-ready, and resilient and to transition between online and offline working easily?

3. To what extent does the job-based approach facilitate continuous learning and upskilling of blended teams? If not, is there a better approach?

Watch out:

Careers for life are a thing of the past! The only sure thing we can count on is continuous change. We need to equip people in our organisations to think and act independently and to adapt to the ever-evolving business context readily. This continuous change also requires a fresh new approach to learning and development, one that considers the increasing fluidity of a blended workforce, resources available to individuals outside of corporate learning structures, and the skills-based role needs that should be prioritised in learning terms. This is for all employees, regardless of designation, location, and level.

The OpenHR challenge:

In our OpenRules chapter, we highlighted the need to create a blended workforce initiative and its role in reviewing the company's talent needs. Firms worldwide recognise the limitations of traditional job structures, yet these have become so deeply embedded in our approach to people management that convincing key stakeholders to move towards more adaptable and effective work approaches won't be an easy task. HR leaders and managers must now rethink not only the way they source talent but also how they organise work as a whole. In pursuing such evolution, both leaders and managers will also need support.

The OpenSkills Room:

When we first set out writing this book, our intention was to highlight a set of hard and soft skills that would be needed within all firms to help them thrive in the post-pandemic 'new world of work.' While this still remains a key part of the vision, we also recognise that ongoing advancements mean that the skills needed at specific periods in the organisation's life cycle will continue to shift. Hence, in our OpenSkills room, we highlight not only hard skills that will remain relevant in the 2020s but also the human-centred power skills that will allow leaders and talent alike to evolve as the business environment continues to demand new knowledge.

Developing the Right Mindset

The shift from a job-based model to a more project or skills-based approach goes against how most HR professionals have been taught to organise people management. Hence, the evolution of the workforce means that not only firms will have to adapt, but educational institutions and professional training bodies will also have to review and update their learnings to navigate wider business shifts. In the past decade, businesses have already begun crying out and seeking external consultants to help them address shifting work expectations. For example, many leaders have been lamenting that they are unable to effectively engage and retain their younger generations of talent, who, on average, stay with one firm for two to three years. Millennials and Generation Z have been pushing back against presenteeism, 'hustle culture,' and jobs-for-life as they pursue happiness and work that is both interesting and meaningful. Research supports this, with Deloitte's Global 2024 Gen Z and Millennials Survey[41] finding that most Gen Zs (86%) and millennials (89%) say having a sense of purpose is crucial to their overall job satisfaction and well-being. In line with our research (The Blended Workforce Revolution[42]), Deloitte also found that these generations were more and more willing to refuse assignments or employers who didn't align with their values. As digital natives, millennials and Gen Z are also more able to leverage technology to earn enough money to sustain their preferred livelihood in a fraction of the time that it took previous generations (e.g. Baby Boomers). Hence, convincing them of the value of staying with one firm and climbing the career ladder for twenty-plus years, while they also observe organisational burnout in older and more senior colleagues, is proving difficult for many companies. Flexibility and work-life balance also remain top priorities for these generations as they seek to pursue other external interests. Hence, organisations' engagement challenges become more obvious when acknowledging these factors.

---

41 https://www.deloitte.com/global/en/issues/work/content/genz-millennialsurvey.html

42 https://www.crowdpotential.co.uk/the-gighr-experts

On top of the above management woes, firms are now expected to respond much faster to global changes, which include sudden economic and environmental shocks, as well as changing market and customer demands. These changes require multi-faceted knowledge and skills that range across different contexts and the capabilities to leverage these in a shorter window of opportunity. In many cases, in-house employees already possess a range of knowledge and skills but have not been encouraged or given the opportunity to apply them to organisational scenarios.

Linear job descriptions and siloed departmental operations often result in the underutilization or wilting of adjacent skills, as employees focus primarily on completing specific roles in the way that they have always approached them. This is also true for our organisational leaders, including HR professionals.

Hence, rather than asking why younger generations are questioning and pushing back against the status quo, leaders should be asking themselves why they have never done the same.

If business leaders want to be able to leverage of technological and societal advancements, then they must begin to truly embrace change by rethinking existing approaches to problem-solving and work organisation. To do this, they themselves need reskilling, upskilling, and organisational support.

INTERVIEW WITH TILO SEQUIERA

To further understand shifting trends and organisational learning and development needs, we spoke to Tilo Sequeira, an experienced international learning and development director for organisations such as Warner Bros., Spotify, and AXA. Tilo has developed and spearheaded several impactful learning and organisational development, talent, and DEI initiatives across mature and emerging markets. Hence, she is best placed to further inform our conjecture on the ongoing developmental needs of firms in the current business environment. Below are extracts from our conversation with her on this subject:

Jeremy Blain and Dr Rochelle Haynes: How do the modern workplace and the rise of the blended workforce impact skills development for the future?

Tilo Sequiera: I read this article about the "Passion Economy," and it is fascinating because it's all about monetizing individuality. What's interesting for me here is the idea that with the rise of online marketplaces, individuals no longer need to stay "tied" to a particular job or commit to a specific career path. The time they were spending in one job can now be spent on multiple "gigs," optimising for a level of flexibility without compromising on earnings. In fact, they are likely earning a lot more than the average permanent worker at the same skill levels.

Jeremy Blain and Dr Rochelle Haynes: So, what does this mean for HR, Talent and Learning professionals everywhere?

Tilo Sequiera: Here are some trends I can foresee in the future for us as a community of Learning and OD experts to keep in mind:

- **The very definition of "permanent employee" is going to change** – Everyone I know has a side hustle these days. They might be working a full-time job. But it has become very common for folks to pursue and monetize other aspects of their worlds outside of work. As such, I feel we will need to redefine and assess if the word "permanent" as we know it today will even hold the same relevance.

- **The pace of and the demand for skills development is going to change as we know it fundamentally** – In the past, you could have someone join a company and continue to do the same job for 10-15- 20 years with no significant delta in real skills. Today, the expectations have changed. It's all about providing just-in-time, bite-sized learning that is also a personalised experience.

- **More Focus on T-shaped Skill Sets and Mindsets** – as the workforce gets more and more complex, individuals will need to focus on both generalist and specialist skill sets. We are seeing this already now, where the focus is shifting from building skills to building mindsets. My opinion on this is that if you have the right mindset, you can build any skill you like!

- **Heightened focus on analytics and working with data** – All functions will redefine their relationship with data and analytics, which means a massive upskilling of teams that did not function with a data-driven mindset in the past

- **More value for L&D and OD skills compared to generalist HR skills** – I anticipate that a lot of HR generalist skill sets are going to get automated over the next decade, so human behaviour and specialist skill sets will take centre stage. Change management and transformation-related skill sets will become highly valuable in HR alongside People analytics and employee experience.

Jeremy Blain and Dr Rochelle Haynes: What can HR professionals and learning experts do to support and build on these shifts?

Tilo Sequiera: There are four key points I'd like to make on this:

1. **Know what problems we are trying to solve** – The needs analysis processes will need to become shorter, sharper, and more frequent to keep up with the pace of learning. Design processes and methodologies that are highly iterative and flexible. They should allow for constant realignment with the ever-changing reality.

2. **Consider mobilising talent with Internal marketplaces** – Internal marketplaces mobilising talent within companies can be a great way to keep both permanent and independent workers engaged and fulfilled. This could be a dynamic marketplace that matches the supply of talent and demand for jobs both short-term and long-term. Many companies have already started this journey.

3. **Focus more on building the right mindsets** – Growth Mindset, grit, change agility, learning agility, habit science, and mental health-related learning will replace the traditional concept of "soft skills development," where the focus in the past has largely been on communication, influencing, and self-leadership skills.

   This will be a welcome change because, like I said before, having the right mindset means you can pick up any skill you like. It is just a question of hard work, willingness to learn, and ability to put in the time. Rather than being constrained by the company you are working with, the role and perceived expectations in skills terms for someone in that job only.

4. **One Common Employee Experience** - No difference in employee experience between permanent and independent workers – We need to ensure one smooth employee experience across all types of workers. Of course, compensation structures might differ based on the work to be done. However, everything else across the employee value chain, like onboarding, access to learning and growth, and benefits, should be the same for all.

Jeremy Blain and Dr Rochelle Haynes: Finally, Tilo, what traits would upgrade HR or L&D professional models for success?

Tilo Sequiera: There needs to be a major reskilling and upskilling of HR professionals in many organisations. This is both a challenging time and an exciting time for us in HR, as we are going to have to work hard to stay ahead of the curve. Top skills I think HR and L&D teams could benefit from in the future:

- Strong Business partnering to have clear needs analysis outputs.

- Change Management & Transformation know-how for the OpenHR(c) era.

- HR 4.0: Digital skill sets and human capital management evolution in line with transformational trends of today…and for tomorrow.

- Data-driven decision making/mindset + Being able to produce insights from Data.

- How to build Experiences – having people feel a certain way after interacting with your employer brand + all HR folks having a basic understanding of human and organisational behaviour

- "Jugaad" is a term we use in India. It means a flexible approach to problem-solving that uses limited resources in an innovative way.

The above insights are indeed in line with our research findings and wider musings. Her experience in developing skills frameworks for the modern workplace and workforce provided us with added perspectives on the key messages in this chapter. In the following sections, we go on to unpick the implications of the above-mentioned changes for organisations that want to take advantage of technological advancements and increase access to globally dispersed expertise and talent.

THE OPENSKILLS ROADMAP: PHYGITAL SKILLS

In our OpenSkills, we have used the word 'Phygital' to describe the important intersection and blend of digital and human capabilities necessary for companies to develop and leverage their blended workforce effectively. In the digital age, the key to successful transformation lies not just in adopting new technologies but in harnessing the full potential of both digital and human capabilities.

As companies introduce new technologies and systems, it is crucial to recognize that technology alone is not enough. True transformation occurs when employees possess a mix of digital proficiency and human-centric skills. Developing and engaging a blended workforce requires digital transformation, which involves integrating digital technologies into all areas of a business, fundamentally changing how companies operate and deliver value to customers. Human skills remain indispensable to the success of this process.

Developing Digital Capabilities

Our blended workforce white paper[43] also revealed that many business and HR leaders surveyed did not possess the digital skills required to manage their independent workforce effectively. HR professionals, particularly, need to consider how they can further embed technological capabilities into the work process if they are to stay ahead. Similarly, many freelancers and in-house employees also need further digital skills development in order to engage clients at a human level better, stay on top of their workflow, and expand their business opportunities.

---

43   https://www.crowdpotential.co.uk/the-gighr-experts

Enhanced digital skills are no longer a 'nice-to-have' option for HR and business leaders. If companies are to benefit from, rather than be victims of, evolving work trends, it is imperative that they adjust the way they work to align with the business culture of the 2020s and 2030s. Particularly, the increasing use of AI and the rise of Gen AI will continue to grow, and HR leaders must find ways to incorporate such technology into their day-to-day operations and practices while encouraging talent to do the same.

As they develop their blended workforce skills, they can begin to meet specific and increased demands for HR-digital integration with open talent. Indeed, our research has shown that many organisations that lack the necessary internal digital capabilities are turning to freelancers to fill this skills gap as they bring their departments up to speed. Among freelance talent, the demand is often highest for those with digital/IT skills, and companies contract independent workers with the necessary expertise to address business needs.

HR must also seek to enhance their digital capabilities so that they have an acute understanding of the digital tools used by their independent workforce. For example, they should be acquainted with digital skills that enhance collaboration, engagement, and interconnectivity.

Leaders and managers alike should be familiar with contemporary work tools to meet different talent needs and remove any feelings of inequity in work interactions. Inspired and transformational management combined with the right digital capabilities will result in the development of a digitally driven culture which embeds a human touch and empowers their blended workforce without prejudice.

To achieve this, HR must begin re-assessing their own training needs by first identifying where the digital gaps in knowledge exist and developing and maintaining an up-to-date knowledge database of these capabilities. From there, these can be prioritised, and leaders can begin assessing the best way to meet these needs.

Essential Digital Capabilities include the following:

1. **Technical Proficiency:** Employees must have a solid understanding of the digital tools and platforms that drive modern business operations. This includes knowledge of data analytics, cybersecurity, cloud computing, and other technological competencies relevant to their roles.

2. **Data Literacy:** The ability to interpret and utilise data effectively and strategically is critical. Employees must be adept at analysing data to make informed decisions, predict trends, and derive actionable insights that can drive business strategy.

3. **Adaptability to New Technologies:** The digital landscape is ever evolving. Employees must be open to learning and adapting to new technologies as they emerge, ensuring that the business remains agile and innovative.

4. **Future/Now knowledge and know-how:** Consider the impending explosion of Generative AI, Blockchain and how that is enabling an acceleration of Web3. Consider the new human power skills that require more than just superficial skills building. For example: Agile collaboration, distributed leadership know-how, enhanced communication and interpersonal toolkits; higher levels of emotional and social intelligence and more.

Digital Toolkit for HR Professionals:

So, we know one of the biggest questions business leaders will have is what digital skills and tools they should focus on to enhance expertise in this area. One of the most obvious is knowledge of AI and Generative AI, which will reshape how leaders lead, impact organisational workflows, automate some jobs, and subsequently drive wider organisational change. Hence, the HR functions should begin experimenting with its different uses to improve productivity and management workflow. AI tools allow HR to automate repetitive and time-consuming elements of their job and frees managers and staff to focus on more strategic activities. Tools like ChatGPT4, for example, have almost two hundred and fifty million users worldwide and allow its users to create templates and written documents and solve problems simply by asking questions. Also, using AI and cloning process, our colleagues at Leonardo Laboratories have designed AI video avatars that can be used for online training or helping HR professionals build and leverage their personal brand. As such technology continues to evolve rapidly, managers are challenged to remain up-to-speed on organisational use cases and to experiment and integrate these AI tools to develop innovative processes. We've outlined below four categories that HR leaders should include in their digital toolkits:

1. COLLABORATION AND COMMUNICATION TOOLS:

A suite of different digital apps/platforms that facilitate different types of communication and collaboration. Leaders should make clear which apps/channels facilitate different types of collaboration:

- Social & Collaboration: Slack, Chanty, Jostle, Social Recognition

- Check-ins: Basecamp, Conversations

- Virtual Meetings: Microsoft Teams, Zoom,

- Team Project: Trello, Asana, Miro, Monday.com,

- Instant Messaging: WhatsApp, Teams

2. CLOUD-BASED SERVICES:

Allows organisations to access HR applications and software on-demand from remote data centres and scale as needed. These typically operate on a subscription-based model, removing the need for significant initial investments. They also offer data analytics, some utilising AI and machine learning to offer performance and talent insights that support key decision-making.

3. HR INFORMATION SYSTEMS

Provide online databases to store talent information and manage their organisational journey. Examples include:

- **BambooHR**: One-stop shop for managing the employee lifecycle.

- **Deel**: Great for managing freelance talent.

- **Sage HR**: Workforce management system suitable for small to medium-sized firms

- **Rippling:** Great for managing a global workforce

Data Analytics Software

These increasingly use machine learning AI (including Gen AI) to help firms predict employee behaviours based on received data.

- **E.g.,** Tableau, Qlik Sense, Zoho Analytics, Microsoft Power BI, Google Analytics, SAP Analytics Cloud

Open Talent Platforms

Digital platforms that allow freelancers to advertise and offer their services to clients and allow companies to source, hire, and manage freelancers according to their specific needs. Many of these offer additional HR-related services to help firms manage freelance relationships. Besides the previously mentioned Fiver and Upwork, other examples include:

- **Gigged.AI**: Allows firms to source, hire and quickly onboard freelance talent with IT skills. Also provides internal talent marketplace services.

- **Toptal:** Exclusive network of top freelance talent across different industries

- **Talmix:** Allows companies to source the best business talent globally.

- **Yuno Juno:** Lets the firm source creative individuals for projects.

- **LinkedIn and LinkedIn Services:** LinkedIn is not traditionally seen as a freelance platform, but it is increasingly allowing firms to source freelancers according to their individual specialisms.

4. MARKETING AND SOCIAL MEDIA

With younger generations making up more of the workforce, HR must get familiar with social media apps and how their talent uses them. Also, they increasingly need to understand how to market themselves or the company as a brand online to attract the right talent and business opportunities. Well-known apps used by employees to build their brand include TikTok, LinkedIn, Snapchat, and Instagram.

5.   MENTAL HEALTH AND WELLNESS:

With employee burnout rising since the COVID-19 pandemic, encouraging positive mental health and wellness has become a top priority for HR. Several apps are designed to encourage individuals to manage their own well-being journey. Some of these include:

- **Headspace:** Science-backed app. Provides mindfulness and meditation exercises and tools for stress reduction

- **Calm:** Focuses on providing good sleep for its users

- **Unmind:** Mental health platform. Encourages employees to improve their mental well-being proactively.

These digital capabilities are now a must to empower the HR function truly, and firms, through consultation with their blended workforce initiative (or champions), should select which tools in each category best fit wider organisational and talent needs. However, digital transformation of the HR function must go hand-in-hand with human transformation. To truly re-imagine the workforce, whole business transformation should remain the real goal in better preparing companies and their people to adapt and leverage relentless change.

Hence, regardless of the specific tools chosen, leaders must become skilled at applying and navigating this technology with purpose and a 'big picture' mindset. In Performance Works' and Bridges' latest research study, The Digital Leadership 2024 Perspective, findings indicated that leaders globally are becoming more digitally confident and adopting new measures as they reap the benefits and efficiencies of incorporating new digital knowledge and tools.

On the flip side, while under great pressure to increase their digital knowledge, many leaders were still missing the purpose of digital transformation. This usually resulted in misaligned investments, objectives, and results.

This brings to mind the 2020 digital transformation rush by companies shifting to remote work and seeking to introduce as many digital tools into their organisations as possible. The result was often duplication, wasted resources, and digital fatigue. This has not changed significantly with several renowned institutions and sources, including Raconteur, McKinsey, BCG, KPMG, and Deloitte, highlighting the alarming 80 to 90% projected failure rate of digital transformation across firms.

Many employees fear and reject change because of a lack of awareness and understanding and because business leaders do not make it clear how changes align with the wider business outcomes. Also, the pace at which the change is being introduced within the company outstrips the current capabilities of employees to utilise it both operationally and strategically. Unfortunately, this is also usually true for the leaders who advocate for and introduce new measures. Business and HR leaders who want to benefit from technological advancements like open talent marketplaces and other digital developments must intentionally pursue transforming their people. We explore this further in the following section.

DEVELOPING HUMAN CAPABILITIES

While the digital toolkit outlined above focuses on the harder, more functional skills, enhancing human capabilities requires developing softer skills. In pursuing the enhancement of digital and human capabilities, businesses must keep the goal of whole business transformation at the forefront before any training endeavours or introduction of new processes begin. Leaders should constantly refer to their wider business objectives and future workforce strategy to understand what they are trying to achieve and determine how and where to invest their time and resources. To do this, they themselves will need support. Leaders must have the skills to leverage digital tools, align these to organisational strategic objectives, build the right internal culture for digital transformation, and empower their people to experiment and effectively implement new tools.

LEADERSHIP DEVELOPMENT

Technological advancement and the rise of this new digital age demand that leaders refill their developmental toolbox with new competencies if they are to drive strategy and influence the behaviour of their workforce. We have outlined some steps below that will help HR leaders identify and pursue developmental needs for their blended workforce:

- Conduct a leadership development assessment.

  - Using their business objectives and future workforce strategy, business leaders should identify the skills needed to achieve the outlined business goals and outline a competency assessment framework that aligns with their specific needs.

  - Conduct an internal leadership competency assessment using the competency framework to diagnose the extent of the skills gap and the specific competencies needed.

  - Categorise these according to business priority.

- Decide which training and development approaches should be used for developing leaders.

- Create a developmental plan for internal talent to equip them to take on future leadership roles.

- Design feedback and measurement metrics and tools to monitor the effectiveness of training.

When measuring the development of these skills, HR leaders need to use a mixture of task- and behaviour-focused metrics. In a hybrid world, they must ensure that as leaders, they can engage and motivate talent working across different mediums so that those working online don't feel invisible and or like second-class citizens. Any measurements used should capture different elements of leaders' development and performance as a whole. Key leadership capabilities that will be needed to engage a blended workforce and transform organisations effectively include:

- **A Growth Mindset** – See challenges as opportunities for growth. Commitment to continuous learning and development through both formal and experiential learning.

- **Self-leadership** – The ability to continuously reflect on, develop and improve your approach to leading.

- **Agility/Adaptability** – Seamlessly adapting to different situations and being ready to handle different challenges.

- **Transformational Leadership** – The power to engage, influence, and motivate different groups of talent to give their best towards the achievement of organisational goals.

- **Change Management** – Effectively leading change initiatives in a way that achieves organisational goals while talent to transition to new processes smoothly.

- **Emotional Intelligence** - Being intuitive to and managing your own and others' emotions. Technology cannot replace the nuanced understanding of human emotions and interactions. Emotional intelligence enables employees to manage relationships effectively, resolve conflicts, and foster a collaborative work environment.

- **Cross-cultural Leadership** - The ability to effectively communicate and coordinate the efforts of persons from diverse cultural backgrounds towards a common objective.

Strong leadership is non-negotiable when guiding teams through the uncertainties of digital transformation. Leaders must inspire and motivate their teams, provide a clear vision, and champion a culture of continuous improvement and innovation. Business and work transformation involves significant changes that will undoubtedly be unsettling for employees. However, transformational leaders can provide a clear vision and roadmap, helping employees understand the purpose and benefits to be gained from present and impending disruption. When achieved, this clarity will help to reduce internal resistance and enhance alignment between the goals of organisations and their people. The next section outlines how companies can reduce some of the inertia associated with wider organisational change through upskilling their talent.

EMPOWERING EMPLOYEES THROUGH UPSKILLING:

In an era where technological advancements are reshaping industries at an unprecedented pace, businesses face a dual challenge: staying competitive and ensuring their workforce is not left behind. The fear of job loss due to automation, artificial intelligence, and other digital developments poses a significant concern among employees.

Added to this is companies' increasing use of open talent in the organisation, which increases companies' access to globally dispersed talent and further elevates in-house talent's fears of being replaced. The reality of technological disruption is not just a future possibility but a present reality. While these advancements promise increased efficiency and new business opportunities, they also pose a threat to jobs that involve routine and repetitive tasks. However, companies can transform these fears into opportunities through strategic upskilling initiatives, where employees can expand their existing capabilities and skill sets.

There are several benefits to pursuing upskilling initiatives on the road to developing your blended workforce. These include.

1. **Boosts Job Security and Employee Morale**

    ○ Ensuring that employees remain relevant in their roles reduces fears of redundancy, enhances feelings of job security and future employment prospects, and increases morale and engagement, leading to a more productive and positive workplace environment.

2. **Bridges Skills Gap**

    ○ As technology evolves, upskilling helps bridge this gap, equipping employees with the necessary competencies to leverage new tools and methodologies. This not only enhances individual career growth but also addresses the talent shortage.

3. **Enhanced Innovation and Adaptability**

    ○ Employees who are well-versed in the latest technologies can contribute to innovation within the company. Upskilling fosters a culture of continuous learning and adaptability, essential traits for navigating the dynamic business landscape.

4. Increased Organisational Competitiveness

- Companies that invest in upskilling their workforce position themselves as leaders in their industry. A skilled workforce is a competitive advantage, enabling businesses to implement new technologies seamlessly and stay ahead of market trends.

Being effective within a blended team does not come naturally to full-time in-house employees, who are now increasingly expected to work more independently and across different time zones and cultures. Employers can easily focus on the here and now in a remote work environment and neglect planning for the long-term employee experience. Leaders must commit to providing their staff with professional growth, career development opportunities, and supporting resources. Regular coaching, feedback, check-ins, and online learning methods (e-learning, training tools, and courses) ensure your employees have something to look forward to as their careers progress. This is a movement from a performance management mentality to one of performance support, which enables a flatter structure for up-and-down-the-line mutualised collaboration.

Many skills employees will need to develop overlap with the leadership skills highlighted in earlier sections (agility, emotional intelligence, self-leadership, growth mindset). Other Indispensable human capabilities that leaders must possess and cultivate in their internal talent pool are:

1. Critical Thinking and Problem-Solving:

- While machines can process vast amounts of data, human intuition and critical thinking are essential for interpreting complex scenarios, making strategic decisions, and solving problems creatively.

2. **Communication Skills:**

   ◦ Clear and effective communication is vital for the successful implementation of digital initiatives. Employees must be able to articulate ideas, share knowledge, and collaborate seamlessly across departments and with stakeholders.

3. **Project Management and Agile Methodologies**

   ◦ Familiarity with project management and agile approaches will help HR better manage and engage open talent and blended team initiatives by increasing efficiency and delivering HR or project solutions that meet business needs. It will also improve employees' ability to innovate and deliver solutions in faster timelines.

By investing in their employee's growth and development, companies mitigate the risk of obsolescence and empower their people to harness the full potential of technological advancements. Upskilling transforms the challenge of technological disruption into an opportunity for innovation, growth, and sustained success. Embracing this approach ensures that employees and businesses thrive in the ever-evolving digital landscape.

STRATEGIES FOR EFFECTIVE UPSKILLING

Organisations can take several approaches to developing both the digital and human (or Phygital) capabilities mentioned in this chapter. The best training initiatives combine several different approaches to accommodate the varying learning styles and abilities of different workers. Strategies for the effective upskilling and re-skilling of talent include:

1. **Comprehensive Training Programs and Micro-Learning**

    - Implement diverse training programs that cater to different learning styles and career stages. These can include workshops, online and bite-sized courses, certifications, and hands-on projects.

2. **Coaching, Mentorship and Peer Learning**

    - Encourage mentorship programs where experienced employees guide their peers. Peer learning fosters a collaborative environment and allows knowledge to be shared organically.

    - Providing leaders and managers with a coach who can encourage and share development, and reflective strategies can help talent with career progression and enhance job prospects.

3. **Flexible Learning Opportunities**

    - Provide flexible learning options that allow employees to learn at their own pace. This can include access to e-learning platforms, webinars, and part-time courses that fit their schedules.

4. **Recognition and Incentives:**

    - Recognize and reward employees who actively participate in upskilling initiatives. Incentives can range from certifications and promotions to bonuses and public recognition. These can be particularly valuable to external talent, who often can't take advantage of firms' full range of training and development opportunities.

5. **Continuous Feedback and Assessment:**

   ◦ Regularly assess the effectiveness of upskilling programs through feedback and performance metrics, as well as more informal communication with different types of talent. This ensures that the training aligns with employee needs and organisational goals.

6. **Cross-Functional Teams**

   ◦ Encourage forming cross-functional teams that bring together individuals with different skill sets. This promotes a culture of collaboration and innovation, leveraging diverse perspectives to drive digital transformation.

The above list represents general approaches to training and development used by organisations. However, these should be adapted to suit the specific context and needs of different firms as well as different groups of talent. As mentioned in the OpenRules, the classification of different types of workers may determine the uptake of different learning offerings provided.

Additionally, the 'workstyle[44]' of open talent, who typically work remotely and have several clients, means that training approaches that take up significant time and require physical attendance would not be appropriate for this group of workers. Hence, the characteristics and needs of different talent groups should be considered. Providing access and discounted voucher codes to independent online short-courses and training platforms like Coursera or Udemy could be alternative solutions, but firms should always consult first with

---

44   https://www.workstylerevolution.com

legal compliance or their blended workforce initiative. The following section addresses how we can provide ongoing support for the HR function, which is often tasked with this ongoing navigation and talent management.

SUPPORTING THE EVOLUTION: HR FOR HR

Constant ongoing shifts in the work environment have taken a toll on the HR profession, which is usually tasked with initiating new organisational mandates, such as the transition to remote work. On top of this, there is a very heavy emotional component to their job roles that senior leaders often overlook. Since the pandemic, HR professionals have had to terminate employees in bulk, comfort staff members who have lost friends and family members, deal with the pain of losing co-workers to suicide and help support burnout co-workers, all while managing their own mental health. This side of the Human Resource Management profession is not highlighted or taught in universities. Julie Turney brought attention to these issues in her book '*Confessions of an HR Pro: Stories of Defeat & Triumph*'[45], where she described HR professionals as organisations' 'unsung heroes' and highlighted key areas in which firms can better support the well-being and development of their HR teams. These include:

1. Provide dedicated time and space for HR professionals to support each other. Having a safe space to discuss challenges and get advice from other HR colleagues is invaluable.

2. Offer training, coaching and mentoring opportunities to help HR professionals grow in their careers and stay motivated. Continuous learning and development are important.

---

45   https://amzn.eu/d/6Mae6b6

3. Watch for signs of burnout and overwork in HR teams. Encourage employees to take proper breaks and time off. HR professionals often neglect their own well-being while supporting others.

4. Ensure HR teams have a manageable workload and sufficient resources to handle their demands. Burnout often stems from unrealistic expectations and a lack of support.

Leaders must recognize this challenge, take proactive steps to support their HRM teams and make a long-term commitment to the well-being of their HR leaders and staff. Leaders must continuously seek ways to enhance the work environment and reduce stressors. By doing so, they not only improve the well-being of HR professionals but also enhance the overall health and productivity of the organisation. HR professionals, or staff with designated HR functions, are the backbone of any organisation, playing a critical role in maintaining a positive and productive workplace. As leaders, we support them, alleviate their workloads, and prevent burnout. By implementing the necessary strategies to ensure and enhance their well-being, we can ensure that our HR teams remain engaged, motivated, and capable of driving the organisation forward.

OPENSKILLS: WHERE TO BEGIN

As with the other Open room, firms should begin their OpenSkills journey with introspection, reflecting on how developing Phygital skills will align their blended workforce initiative with overall organisational objectives. Therefore, we recommend that leaders begin with the OpenSkills self-evaluation questionnaire outlined below:

OpenSkills Roadmap: Self-Evaluation Questionnaire:

Self-Evaluation Questions:	Answers
When did you last update your library or database of 'team member' skills for full-time staff?	
What exists as a similar database of skills/capabilities you need possessed by external recruitment or open talent companies that you may have previously worked with?	
How up to date is your learning needs analysis approach? And how does it cater for the new knowledge, skills, and behaviours required by all employees, regardless of whether they are permanent employees or otherwise?	
When did you last create a glossary of new tools and skills explaining what they are and what is expected from each person at all levels? Is it up to date with the needs of the 2030s workforce and the steps and skills required now?	
What skills gaps exist between your companies and contractor pool, and how might this affect future organisational needs and priorities?	
How wide or narrow is the capability gap between your leaders and employees when considering digital era skill sets and ways of working and collaborating? How does this offer opportunities for flatter management structures and greater all-level mutual support and collaboration?	
What are the current digital skills/readiness levels among your existing permanent and open workforce?	

How capable are your senior-most organisational and functional leaders in terms of knowledge, behaviours, and skills when considering digital-era skill sets?	
What parameters currently exist to support your open workforce during project engagement?	
What does the next iteration of your performance management process and approach look like for both permanent and independent workers?	

Chapter 7

OPENTHRILLS: THE FOURTH ROOM

Figure 6: The OpenThrills Room

The art of catching people doing it right and building forward momentum for the continuing journey.

Goal:

To create the new DNA for the organisation that mobilises, engages, motivates, and commits employees at all levels (both permanent and independent workers) to the journey ahead.

THE OPENHR KEY QUESTION

How do we support our re-invigorated human-centred framework through creating a connected, collaborative, mutually supportive, recognition-centred culture?

Watch out:

If we do everything else but do not have the structures in place to properly recognise and reward our people for a more connected, collaborative, joined-up effort, all our good work to this point will evaporate as the rest of the organisation asks, 'So what?' and becomes increasingly disillusioned.

THE OPENHR CHALLENGE

Championing the organisation as a great place to be, with a strong culture of collaboration, mutual support, recognition, and reward.

> **The art of creating a mobilised, engaged, motivated workforce, which is recognised and rewarded for the new behaviours it embraces and the results it achieves.**

Any organisation committed to implementing the OpenHR framework in its entirety and at all levels relies on a more connected, mobilised, and engaged workforce. With this in mind, those charged with leading the implementation of the framework must think through how to underpin all the components with a robust recognition and reward structure. This structure should catch people doing it right, highlighting new behaviours, emerging skills, and those making an impact within and beyond their job roles as they contribute to broader business health.

Having a thought-through recognition and reward structure will help to minimise our 'watch out' highlighted at the beginning of this section. That of a disillusioned, disengaged workforce ready to vote with its feet.

Instead, we can value the organisational change desired at all levels. This will ensure those committing to the new journey and understanding the principles of the OpenHR approach will develop and grow with the company, not apart from it.

They will feel part of the journey, appreciate being in a more connected, collaborative environment, and welcome a culture where the new behaviours, actions, results, and so on are recognised and rewarded, not just taken for granted.

For many, this will represent an ideal situation, as they no longer feel the pressure or need to be merely individual contributors. Instead, they become part of a more joined-up, collective response to protecting business health. It's more motivating, engaging, and rewarding for everyone. This is where OpenThrills comes of age.

Below are some tactics to consider as the organisation formalises its recognition and reward approach. This should be the starting point and will spark additional ideas suited to the organisation and individuals concerned. These are also listed in Jeremy Blain's book, 'Unleash the Inner CEO - Make Distributed Leadership a Reality'[46] and reproduced with kind permission from the author here:

---

46   https://performanceworks.global/theinnerceo/

Recognition and reward suggestions to add to your own

	Ideas and suggestions					
How to effectively recognize people / effort	Senior leadership team meeting presentation	Certification system (bronze, silver and gold in-role CEOs) based on specific measurable / provable criteria that all those unleashing their inner CEO can aspire to	Gamify the unleashing of the inner CEOs > badges / merits linked to non-monetary awards (i.e. lifestyle awards)	Appointing an executive leader mentor to accompany the journey for specific projects or points in time	Inclusion in relevant strategic meetings, special projects and external events	Announcements in company events, newsletters and with customers.
Non-monetary reward	Time off for wellness and personal pampering	Party or awards event for the individual and their team / collaborative group	Paid dinner for the individual with friends / partner / family	Paid holiday for the individual and their family / partner	Learning and development to grow strategic / leadership skills (outside of normal learning path)	Trips and visits to other parts of the company (globally) to share best practices and experiences
Monetary rewards	Bonus based on qualitative and quantitative impact on the business and other stakeholders (rewarding both behaviours and results)	Annual increases in salary, on top of normal increase, possible up to an incremental percentage defined by the business (such as an additional 5% based on in-role CEO performance)	Bonus payment on attaining bronze, silver, gold certification as in-role CEO	Line manager discretionary budget to provide relatively small monetary bonuses during regular reviews throughout the year	CEO Special Award – a competition in parallel with other activities to identify and reward the best new initiative that has biggest impact on the business, on people and on the customer: a large one-off cash prize and public recognition	New contract / extended contract / long term contract for those *independent freelance workers* contributing with consistency and excellence to the business

Having all this in place up front enables people to buy in fully to the OpenHR journey, helping you shape the new organisation across permanent employees, independent workers, and contractors.

Some notable examples of how some organisations globally are thinking differently about recognition and reward include:

- Zappos: A peer-to-peer rewards programme transcending traditional organisational reward mechanisms.

- GE Healthcare: Who puts recognition and reward at the heart of change management - catching people doing it right in terms of effort, behaviours, and collaboration.

- E.ON: How is the humble 'thank you' note being used to great effect and with value in employees' eyes, regardless of their designation?

- Apple: Rewarding their workforce internationally with paid time off in recognition of effort, behaviours, and results.

Read how these companies do it in the fabulous article *'4 Companies That Have Nailed Their Employee Recognition Strategy' by* Chiradeep BasuMallick from Spiceworks (September 2023)[47].

Some other great examples that bring creatively, value and personalisation into how a truly blended workforce might be recognised and rewarded are listed below:

1. In the 2021 article in Forbes, *'How are you rewarding your best freelancers'* contributor Jon Younger argues that we need to look after our freelancers and our permanent employees and provides

---

47   https://www.linkedin.com/pulse/4-companies-have-nailed-employee-recognition-strategy-dipali-g-

examples of companies who agree – with actions over words. Including organisations such as Folq, Fintalent and Itarmi.[48]

2. *Creative Access* argues that we can do more for freelancers specifically, especially as they are becoming a formalised part of organisational workforces everywhere. They encourage a consideration of the 'whole person' to recognise effort, lifestyle, workstyle and ongoing skills development and growth.[49]

3. Platforms like Perkpal and Perkbox take down the walls between permanent, part-time, and independent workers. All are part of the team, and the platform allows for a gamified approach to recognition and tagged rewards mechanics for the entire workforce. Regardless of their designation.

4. The workforce payments organisation Branch argues that reward and recognition of independent workers is also about making their lives easier. For example, how they are designated in a particular country (i.e. in the U.S. the 1099 contractors or W-2 employees).[50] In this respect, we would advise you to consider how your company can help with faster payments, taxation data and assistance and more. This kind of recognition is of huge value to independent workers of all designations. But this also means that some businesses need to change in order to better service their blended workforce. For example, the need for a new payment terms policy for freelancers. Why is this a need? Because some freelancers still work for large organisations and sit at 90-day payment terms, like larger suppliers. This is

---

48   https://www.forbes.com/sites/jonyounger/2021/03/29/
      how-are-you-rewarding-your-best-freelancers/

49   https://creativeaccess.org.uk/app/uploads/2024/01/freelancer-re-
      port-final.pdf

50   https://www.branchapp.com/blog/how-to-boost-loyal-
      ty-with-1099-workers#:~:text=Branch%20allows%20you%20to%20
      send,you%20significant%20time%20and%20energy

nonsense in the new world and is not viable for what is likely a highly valuable and valued resource for the company.

5. Vestd in the UK, argues the case for 'non-employees' (for example consultants, advisors, freelancers or other contractors not directly managed by the company) and an approach to reward through providing equity, growth shares and other mechanics to act as both recognition and incentive.[51] This means non-employees have more of a stake and this where value is mutualised and beneficial to all concerned.

6. Compport also considers reward and recognition for non-employees as going beyond one-off incentives or ad hoc bonuses etc. For example, they list the areas below as viable considerations for rewarding and recognising non-employees and provide the detail in their associated article.[52] Some of these include:

- Project-Based Compensation

- Hourly or Daily Rates

- Performance-Based Incentives

- Commission or Revenue-Sharing

- Retainer Agreements

- Equity or Stock Options

- Performance Bonuses

---

51   https://www.vestd.com/blog/
      how-to-reward-advisors-contractors-and-others-with-equity

52   https://www.compport.com/blog/non-employee-compensation-re-
      warding-partners-freelancers-and-contractors

- ○ Professional Development Opportunities

- ○ Recognition and Awards

- ○ Non-Monetary Perks

- ○ Deferred Compensation

- ○ Negotiated Custom Packages

To further exemplify how blended team rewards work practically, **we interviewed Meighan Newhouse, CEO of Inspirant Group,** an award-winning consulting firm headquartered in Chicago. At Inspirant, Meighan spearheaded the development of a culture that embeds independent contractors into their workforce, in a way that creates a united and harmonious work environment, which produces effective results for clients.

Jeremy Blain and Dr Rochelle Haynes: Please give us an example of the practices that your company uses to recognise freelancers?

Meighan: We've heard comments from some of our freelancers, who are new to our company. I have a couple of quotes. "I've never been treated this well by a company, like as a contractor, let alone as a full-time employee." You know that. I mean, people are just kind of pinching themselves. I think it's really how we work together. And one of the gigsters posted on LinkedIn, that we sent her some swag, as we do with anybody who joins the company, so she was singing our praises. That's the whole reason I'm doing what I'm doing. People should love the work they're doing, and I want them to feel part of something and you know, in an organisation where they can really do their best as a permanent employee or as a freelancer. There should be no difference.

Jeremy Blain and Dr Rochelle Haynes: Yes absolutely! Can you tell us a bit more about the communication and integration process and how you navigate these?

Meighan: So, when they are hired, they become an 'unconsultant' before becoming a formalised consultant. And we have a process similar to onboarding; a one-on-one or as a group when many people start at the same time. But regardless, if it's just one person, or if it's six people, we have a deck that we go through. It's nothing too fancy. But our People and Culture lead and our Operations lead go through what it means to be an unconsultant, and that includes covering our core values. Often through different team building activities, which freelancers are welcome to participate in, without any pressure or expectation. Essentially, we want them to feel welcome to participate as part of our overall team.

And we also share basic logistics and processes. It's about an hour, just walking them through and answering questions. It's just another way to introduce them to more of the team as well.

So, part of those team building activities, that all unconsultants are welcome to participate in, is the buddy system. We call them the buddy chats, but every month, we pair up two unconsultants, and they can meet however they want.

So, they could schedule one hour for the month and take that hour in full, or they could do 20 minutes a week. Or if they live near each other, and they're comfortable getting together for a coffee or a drink, or they can get online and play a game together. It doesn't matter.

They get paired up with someone new every month, as a way to get to know the team. And we instantly integrate our new hires into the process as well.

Another thing we have is our Inspirant celebrations. So, the first Thursday of the month, we celebrate the traditional birthdays and anniversaries.

But then we discussed internally and looked at other things to celebrate. It could be a new pet, it could be they bought a new house, it could be they just got certified in something. We just celebrate. And sometimes we send them little gifts.

On the third Thursday of each month is a lunch-and-learn session that everyone is welcome to attend. We either have internal speakers or external speakers on a variety of topics. It is received by permanent employees and non-employees very positively.

We also have quarterly all hands events where we conduct different activities like professional development, social events, team building and more.

Jeremy Blain and Dr Rochelle Haynes: And when you say unconsultants, does that include both your 'gigsters' and your full-time employees?

Meighan: That's exactly right. We came up with that word, because honestly, I don't really want people to be able to tell who's who. To me it doesn't matter. No matter what your tax return says. If you are working for Inspirant, you're part of the team and you're part of the culture.

Jeremy Blain and Dr Rochelle Haynes: How easy have you found it for freelancers to become integrated longer term; for example, as permanent employees?

Meighan: If it was the right person, if we did a good job in those initial conversations, we would offer them a full-time role.

Now, we've been hiring pretty rapidly, and the way we've been most successful growing our team is through existing freelance consultants, either as employees, or through longer term contracts, or as a body referring us to people that they know. We've had a lot of success with that.

In addition, every Wednesday on our company LinkedIn page we started a 'what inspires you' Wednesday post, open to all unconsultants regardless of their employment status. It's a choice and we are mindful that some freelancers have their own businesses and prefer not to be seen as a part of the company, or as a subcontractor. That is fair enough.

We also have a weekly newsletter, open to all; and on Fridays we spotlight one of our unconsultants, typically including photos of their choice alongside a handful of questions they have answered, about them, their work and their role supporting Inspirant.

Finally, we have several company awards, for example, the 'Living Our Values' award, and this is open to all of our unconsultants, including freelancers. It's regarded as high value across all of our workforce.

OPENTHRILLS ROOM - ACTION START POINTS FOR EACH ELEMENT

The table below summarises initial thoughts and ideas as a start point for you to add your own thinking. Across each component within the OpenThrills room.

OpenThrills Key elements	Objectives for each element	Ideas and action (start point)

Connect	Enabling greater cohesion between individuals, teams, and functions internally and with independent contractors and customers externally, through digital technologies.	Bring the tech and touch together by empowering people at all levels to own it – encouraging connections across teams and more widely.
Create	Innovation as the driver of growth >> promotes creativity as the foundation for teams and stakeholders to experiment and create new solutions that win with the customer and across the business.	Establish managers as coaches to encourage ideas and actions at all levels, being the conduit between the leadership and the workforce internally and externally.
Communicate	Create a culture of trust to facilitate open and rapid communication to solve problems, overcome difficulties, and enhance emerging valued practices.	Adopt psychological safety principles to allow for clear lines of communication devoid of politics, power plays, and personal preferences.
Collaborate	Empower our people at all levels to go beyond their job description and work with others in dynamic project groups and teams to support customer, business, and workforce growth.	Adopt agile working methods and upskill the organisation to work collaboratively using the tech, tools, and processes to enable rapid progress and impact.

Celebrate	Recognise and reward our permanent and independent workforce appropriately and fairly for modelling the new valued behaviours and impacting results.	Organisational, functional, managerial, and peer recognition and reward infrastructure with clear rules of the road and dos/don'ts are supported by central ownership of the process.
Cultivate	Embrace a Growth Mindset and build momentum through the actions and activities above to ensure the long-term sustainability of your OpenHR framework and OpenThrills commitments.	Plan ahead to build on early progress and empower the organisation to own OpenThrills progress. For example: • Company sharing portals • CEO awards • Workforce-owned Town Halls • Internal and external surveys/pulse assessments are used to secure action-intended feedback.

Critical questions to answer driving your 90-day implementation plan.

	Questions to answer	Our ideas and 90-day plan action plan
Connect	• What gaps have we in the way our employees, teams and functions connect with each other? • Do we have any existing best practices internally we can work with? • How connected does our permanent and independent workforce feel to the organisation? • How connected do our customers feel to the organisation beyond their day-to-day contacts? • How connected are our other stakeholders (partners, suppliers, and shareholders)?	

Create		
	• How creative are our teams and individuals? • What supporting skills development do we need to put in place to engage our teams in creativity, experimentation, and innovation? • How do we re-purpose line managers to advocate and coach our people? • What will we do to excite our teams behind this drive? • What measurables can we use to track qualitative and quantitative impact?	

Communicate	<ul><li>How would we rate the culture NOW regarding willingness to have open, challenging conversations?</li><li>Do we need to do any trust-building internally and externally? If so, what?</li><li>How do we support individuals and teams in having more challenging/difficult discussions in the right way to unlock co-working, new ideas, and greater openness?</li><li>How can psychological safety underpin our drive to enable more open communications internally and externally?</li><li>How do we encourage greater levels of open communication 'up the line' and at peer level?</li></ul>	

| Collaborate | <ul><li>Can we truly empower our people to work in high-performing collaborative teams?</li><li>What must we do to create high-impact internal and external collaboration conditions?</li><li>How do our external partners and resources collaborate effectively with our internal resources for the good of the business and our customers?</li><li>What does gold-standard collaboration look like within our organisation?</li><li>How do we measure the impact of greater self-driven, collaborative teams in our organisation?</li></ul> | |

<table>
<tr>
<td>Celebrate</td>
<td>

- How do we manage and measure performance in new ways to better recognise both qualitative and quantitative drivers for our business?

- How does our recognition and reward infrastructure evolve to support our new OpenHR framework?

- What can we do to develop recognition and some reward levels for functions, line managers, and collaborative teams to enable a more rapid and meaningful appreciation of high performance and the display of new behaviours we want to embed?

- What can we do at the organisational/executive leader level to call out people and teams getting it right?

- How do we avoid a culture of 'over-reward' if we overhaul this system and devolve some recognition and awards?

</td>
<td></td>
</tr>
</table>

Cultivate	<ul><li>How clear is the organisation, at all levels, on what a growth mindset is and why it is important for our business?</li><li>How do we re-purpose line management to be focused on results delivery alongside the growth of their people at all levels?</li><li>How do we encourage leadership at all levels to move a growth mindset into meaningful action?</li><li>How do we know we are making progress beyond short-term gains and wins?</li><li>Where do we want to be 2 years from now?</li></ul>	

Having all this in place up front enables people to buy in fully to the OpenHR journey as a whole, with the security of knowing there is a robust reward and recognition approach, across the entire workforce regardless of whether that relates to permanent employees, independent workers, and freelance contractors.

Chapter 8

OPENPROTECT: PROTECTING YOUR OPENHOUSE THROUGH WELLBEING AND PERFORMANCE

Figure 7: The OpenProtect Roof

A strong, leak-free roof to secure productivity and performance underpinned by organisational psychological safety protocols.

We spent a lot of time talking about culture being the strongest of foundations. If you are investing heavily in that, the natural extension is to provide extra protection and security for your company and workforce – whether they are permanent or independent workers. This is all about human-centred protection for our times.

As we emerged from the pandemic, many more organisations and executive leaders truly understood the importance of looking after the most important asset – people. Wellbeing, mental health, empathy, emotional intelligence, and more were central to industry news week after week. In fact, in some industries, it has become a competitive advantage in talent attraction and retention. Prospective and current employees and contractors were looking at how the organisation's culture evolved and what checks and balances were implemented to support and upskill workers for remote times. As the hybrid workplace appears to be the new normal, these initial actions can be further reinforced and will become even more important to the ongoing 'War for Talent' and associated trends, as explained by SHRM in their 2024 article: '*7 Trends Defining the Ongoing War for Talent*'[53]

The wellbeing and safety angle is not just a human one, of course. It must respect the distributed nature of work, the need for enabling technologies, and the need for these to fuel seamless collaboration and communication safely while protecting data and people. If the technologies are not fit for purpose, they will overwhelm, create more work, and destroy motivation and productivity. We have seen it repeatedly.

Therefore, as we seek to secure our roof on the OpenHouse, we must understand the most appropriate technologies and how these interact across the entire blended workforce, encompassing both permanent and independent workers.

These technologies combine with strong, compassionate leadership that brings people together. Productivity and performance are enhanced, underpinned by an understanding and active interest in the well-being and mental health of the blended workforce.

---

53   https://www.shrm.org/executive-network/insights/
       seven-trends-defining-ongoing-talent-war-shrm

Let's examine each component in more detail…

WELLBEING AS A DRIVER OF PERFORMANCE AND PRODUCTIVITY

In her 2019 article 'The Link Between Employee Wellbeing and Performance'[54] Donna Griffiths of Westfield Health says:

'Employers are increasingly focusing on wellbeing in the workplace as a key driver in improving company culture. It's becoming clearer that a healthy and happy workforce is more productive, motivated and engaged – ultimately leading to organisational success.'

Our foundation, roof, and component parts all link to create the productivity and performance ecosphere required for workforce success and well-being. It's a powerful combination that reinforces the cultural shift required and the orientation around it to protect, support, and guide the workforce through all its lenses.

This is an important aspect of the new OpenHR framework to master.

- In the UK, according to the Mental Health Foundation, 14.7% of employees suffer mental health issues in the workplace.[55]

- According to Spill, in 2024, 6 out of every 10 workers globally are experiencing workplace stress.[56] That is 60% of the working population. In fact, nearly 1 million employees in the U.S. miss work every day due to stress and mental health issues. These are staggering statistics.

54   https://journals.sagepub.com/doi/10.1177/014920639902500305

55   https://shorturl.at/h3Ou9

56   https://www.spill.chat/mental-health-statistics/
      workplace-stress-statistics

- According to Buffer.com, just over 1 in 5 remote workers suffer from loneliness, which directly impacts their productivity and performance.[57]

THE COST OF NOT BUILDING YOUR PROTECTIVE ROOF

Here are some statistics to take into the boardroom:

According to the World Economic Forum and the Harvard School of Public Health, the cost of mental health conditions is projected to rise to $6 trillion globally by 2030, from $2.5 trillion in 2010.[58]

Another study by the UK Government puts the wider economic costs of mental illness in England alone at an estimated £110 billion each year (around $150 billion USD).[59] This includes direct costs of services, lost productivity at work and reduced quality of life.

Staying with the UK, Forbes estimated that even before the pandemic 91 million workdays were lost in the UK due to symptoms of mental illness. If we extrapolate that across the top 30 economies worldwide, it would be astonishingly high. And it's accelerated since the COVID 19 pandemic of the early 2020s.[60]

Sapien Labs underlined the post pandemic mental health accelerating trends in their 'Mental State of World Report, 2023'. The data are

---

57   https://buffer.com/state-of-remote-work/2023

58   https://intelligence.weforum.org/topics/a1Gb0000000pTDbEAM

59   https://www.centreformentalhealth.org.uk/
wp-content/uploads/2024/03/CentreforMH_
TheEconomicSocialCostsofMentalIllHealth.pdf

60   https://www.forbes.com/sites/katherinehignett/2023/07/28/
mental-illness-keeping-englands-health-staff-off-sick/

cause for concern, with an urgent need t0 understand the continuing impact on our collective mental wellbeing.[61]

Higher instances of mental health and wellness issues impact the longevity of employees who are not treated and supported. This drives higher turnover rates, which means more money is spent on recruitment, hiring, and retraining new employees. Particularly at management or leadership level. A study from SHRM in the US now puts that cost at nearly $15,000 USA to replace just one executive level employee.[62] Now link that to some of the data above and the cost of not doing anything about this becomes incalculable.

THE BENEFITS OF A ROBUST OPENPROTECT APPROACH

According to Haptivate's November 2020 blog '*The Benefits of Wellbeing at Work*,' there are tangible reasons to fast-track an organisation's health, wellness and employee support programmes: 'Happy workers are 20% more productive, 34% less likely to leave their jobs and 37% less likely to take time off sick.'[63]

This indicates the huge benefits in terms of time, money, HR and management focus gained by getting this right – and it is relevant for both permanent and independent workers.

---

61   https://sapienlabs.org/wp-content/uploads/2024/03/4th-Annual-Mental-State-of-the-World-Report.pdf

62   https://resources.workable.com/stories-and-insights/the-cost-of-replacing-an-employee#14936

63   https://haptivate.co.uk/blog/the-benefits-of-wellbeing-at-work-where-to-start-what-works/

According to Wellsteps.com (Employee well-being study[64]), offering employees wellbeing-at-work support several compelling benefits:

1. Improvement in employee health behaviours

2. Reduction of elevated health risks

3. Reduction in health care costs

4. Improvements in productivity

5. Decrease in absenteeism

6. Improvements in employee recruitment and retention

7. Greater ability to build and help sustain high employee morale

A further study by Peppy, shows us the impact of wellbeing programmes in reducing absenteeism by 14-19%, with almost 6 out of every 10 employees having fewer sick days.[65]

Positive actions you can take now to fast-track your OpenProtect approach:

Psychological safety is essential for creating a positive workplace environment where whole person wellbeing, collaborations and communications can happen openly, freely and without judgement.

The first step, therefore, is to think about how psychologically safe your organisation is, and how committed to creating the right climate your executive leaders and line managers are, in reality. Getting it wrong can be disastrous and getting it right can have a much greater

---

64   https://www.wellsteps.com/blog/2020/01/02/
       employee-well-being-at-work/

65   https://shorturl.at/MLoQD

positive impact on the organisation as a whole. For everyone, at all levels, for any designation of employee in your blended working. Primary benefits can include:

a. Enhanced Engagement: Employees feel more motivated and engaged when they know their input is valued.[66]

b. Improving wellbeing and mental health, including lowering day-to-day stress levels: A safe environment significantly reduces anxiety and stress, contributing to employees' overall well-being.[67]

c. Improved Collaboration: Openness encourages team members to share ideas and work together effectively, fostering innovation.[68]

d. Attraction and Retention: Companies that prioritise recruitment efforts.[69]

e. Work-Life Balance: Employees are empowered to establish boundaries, leading to an improved work-life balance.[70]

3. Create a happier, healthier and more open organisational environment by creating wellbeing champions for your entire workforce, across both permanent and independent workers.

---

66   https://hbr.org/2023/02/what-is-psychological-safety

67   https://www.ccl.org/articles/leading-effectively-articles/
      what-is-psychological-safety-at-work/

68   https://www.nhsemployers.org/articles/
      top-tips-supporting-psychological-safety-staff

69   https://corporateculture.co.uk/
      the-5-big-benefits-of-psychological-safety/

70   https://shorturl.at/WAbr1

The Wellbeing project has some great examples and advice in this area, and you can find more details in the footnote.[71]

4. Support your permanent employees with formalised programmes and invite your valued independent workforce to attend and be part of the process.

5. Create a holistic wellbeing policy and programme suite that supports the blended workforce. This may change the traditional ways that human resources have been managed and supported, but it is in step with the evolution of the modern workplace and how people choose to work (and where to work from).

Following your consideration and further reading in our footnotes, think about what you could stop, continue and start doing, in your organisation, to move forward with employee wellbeing in mind. Regardless of level or designation within your blended workforce.

---

71   https://thewellbeingproject.co.uk/insight/wellbeing-champions/

OPENPROTECT

Wellbeing – Productivity – Performance

(make notes to capture ideas and actions)

We need to stop doing	We need to continue doing	We need to start doing

OPENPROTECT

Wellbeing – Productivity – Performance

GETTING TO ACTION

From the links, examples, and ideas in this chapter, discuss the questions below across the organisation and make a note of your initial ideas and targeted actions. You'll then be in good shape to create your ongoing 90-day action plan to implement the best of your ideas and needs.

In-depth discussion points will guide your OpenProtect action plan.

Key Questions	Notes and Ideas	Your 90-Day Action Plan
What does a gold standard wellbeing and mental health policy and support programme look like for our future blended workforce?		
How do we create a psychologically safe climate and culture to allow openness of sharing; especially around whole person wellbeing for our blended workforce?		

What are the wellbeing and safety imperatives arising from the pandemic that will build into our approach going forward?		
What have well-being, safety and mental health issues cost our organisa-tion over the past five years?		
What do we predict wellbeing, safety and mental health issues will cost our organisation over the next five years?		
How do we dramat-ically shift our approach to benefit people, productivity, performance, and profit?		

Who can we learn from within and outside our industry to identify best practices and traps to avoid?		
How do we identify permanent and independent worker champions to represent our work-force and contribute to the way forward?		
What do we expect from these champions, and how do we buy them into the process and recognise their contribution?		
What new policies, rules, and standards may be required at the organisation development (OD) level to encompass the full breadth of the defined blended workforce?		

What support and sponsorship will the board and executive leaders require to fast-track progress?		
How will we measure progress at both quantitative and qualitative levels – from day 1?		
How will we know we are making progress?		
What feedback loops can we implement to allow for rapid communication, idea sharing and corrective action if needed?		

What does it feel like to be part of an organisation with a robust well-being, safety, and mental health approach in place?		
How will this impact the attraction, retention, and growth of our people?		
How do we become the benchmark company in our industry for work-place well-being, mental health, and safety for our entire workforce – both permanent employees and independent workers?		

Workplace well-being, psychological safety, and mental well-being will become competitive advantages for organisations regarding human resources. It will attract prospective employees, help retain existing employees, and make any organisation a sought-after partner for independent workers, contractors, and other external stakeholders.

This benefits the blended workforce and adds a robust, reinforced, rock-solid roof to your OpenHouse.

Now that we have the foundation and the roof in hand, we can start considering the four rooms in our house. This will make our brand new OpenHR human capital management framework a reality.

Chapter 9

IMPLEMENTING AND MEASURING YOUR BLENDED WORKFORCE EFFECTIVENESS AND OPENHR SUCCESS

According to the Strategy Implementation Institute, strategy implementation fails over 65% of the time.[72]

Strategies that are defined well with every piece thought through can fail in these instances as there is little planning for implementation, engaging the rest of the organisation, handling early challenges, creating early wins and crucially building momentum once progress is being made.

This is why we have provided questions to answer and examples to consider as we encourage you to develop your own 90-day plan as you progress through each chapter and each element of our OpenHR framework.

---

72   https://www.strategyimplementationinstitute.org/

But that won't be enough without a robust implementation plan to accelerate progress, build momentum and embed the shift culturally into the organisation and across your blended workforce.

According to MBO Partners 'Contingent Labor Report, 2022,' there are specific reasons why implementing strategies based around workforce mix, specifically hiring of contingent workers, could fail or succeed. The 5 main reasons are the must-dos and most important reasons for hiring and integrating independent workers into a formalised blended workforce. These are wrapped around the need for consistency and the quality of work delivery, as this extract from the report demonstrates[73]:

USING CONTINGENT LABOR

Ranked by Top Reasons Ensuring Consistency of Work Quality

1. 30% - Finding / hiring contingent labour with the skills we need

2. 30% - Getting tasks done more quickly is the promise we need to be delivered

3. 27% - Accessing skill sets in short supply

4. 23% - Accessing talent not available to us

5. 22% - Saving money'

If we can secure all of this for our organisation effectively, we are in great shape to achieve the success we aim for. However, this requires a robust strategic and operational implementation plan to avoid failing before we get started. If any of the above doesn't quite work

---

73   https://www.mbopartners.com/state-of-independence/ contingent-labor-report/

out or fails altogether, it impacts the whole. We have to understand how to get it done at the executive leader level as much as through the rest of the organisation.

Therefore, we offer both a strategic and operational imperatives list to assure implementation success more confidently:

1. Strategic buy-in and structural transformation

2. The operational execution plan, engagement, and measures are in place.

STRATEGIC BUY-IN AND STRUCTURAL TRANSFORMATION - CONSIDERATIONS

- Build your business case for OpenHR. Internally and for servicing your customers even better

- Have a stress-tested strategic plan complete with operational must do's and measures

- Think about how to secure the executive leadership (and board level) mindset shift and buy-in

- Work on the creation of the most suited version of our OpenHouse structure, providing the framework for new processes, technologies and people management for a more open workforce

- Create a bold new governance document, to be developed alongside structural change and signed off at the board/executive leader level

- Ensure there is a senior leader and line management communication plan and reskilling where required

- Provide a simple, clear and exciting statement of intent for employees (existing), independent workers and customers. This ensures customers stay at the heart of your blended workforce focus and OpenHR framework evolution.

- Define roles, responsibilities and ownership of the implementation plan with clear measurables in place from day one to track qualitative and quantitative progress

OPERATIONAL EXECUTION PLAN, ENGAGEMENT AND CONSIDERATIONS

- Establish and distribute your high-level workforce and customer communication plans, complete with clear 'what's in it for us/me' messaging

- Secure visible and clear executive leadership and management sponsorship, stewardship and support in the eyes of the workforce

- Set up a cross-workforce council to be part of the project execution group, with a voice at executive leadership level briefings (including having a senior executive sponsor to work with)

- Always be mindful to include the customer's voice and secure regular feedback from the customer to track improvements or roadblocks to ongoing customer experience promise delivery.

- Underpin **everything** with a psychologically safe foundation to encourage experimentation, evolution and adaptation of the model accordingly, as the implementation plan is executed in line with stated objectives and actions.

- It is critical to have a 90day plan with weekly measurables that all can own driving a more inclusive approach to making your OpenHR framework and execution successful. This can be developed strategically and then across teams as 90day operational plans.

- Make sure you catch people doing it right! Have a plan to recognise and reward positive behavioural change as much as quantitative measures. A major boost for engagement and workforce motivation, as well as a key pivot for culture building.

- Ensure ongoing governance reviews at the board and executive leader level are supported by regular, databacked reporting and any recommended adaptive plans based on the ongoing situation.

Guiding Success:

These considerations represent the red thread for successful strategic planning and operational implementation, particularly when considering other major workplace and business model transformations we have been through recently. We have to demonstrate we have learned from these. We have taken the very best learnings and are mindful of the pitfalls, must-dos and don'ts!

Each element, whether strategic or operational, should be supported by a healthy growth mindset, underpinned by a psychologically safe environment and a 'good culture' approach to enable open and honest communication, formalised feedback, and regular reviews to celebrate early wins and agree on any course corrections that may be required. Everyone is involved in this, regardless of level, to even out the accountability for success across the broader organisation.

Importantly, this will be supercharged by a deconstructed vertical management structure to operate more horizontally, resulting in more empowerment for both the workforce and line management. This will encourage a more collaborative approach to managing others while providing support over supervision, coaching over criticism, transparent, open communication rather than opaque selective sharing, and a greater feeling of community over isolated working or direction.

Reap the Benefits of an OpenHR-Enabled Blended Workforce:

Getting the above strategic and operational elements right will enable success. This is not just from a business 'numbers' perspective but also in that your workforce can operate without the constraints of legacy structures and ways of working. It's more adaptable and helps the organisation deliver short-term results while enjoying greater future readiness at a time where speed of change, innovation and action represent the competitive currency of today.

From our observations when working with enlightened organisations adopting our OpenHR approach, it is clear the top 15 big wins, following feedback from the executive leadership, the blended workforce itself and human resources professionals, are as follows:

- **Flexibility**: OpenHR underpinning a blended workforce will help organisations rapidly adapt to varying workloads and more specialised tasks. Whether opportunity-focused or through the lens of required change or problem-solving.

- **Diverse, Equitable, and Inclusive**: A big win of OpenHR and embracing a blended workforce is that the whole approach brings together a range of expertise and perspectives, regardless of gender, age, employment designation, geography, location, sexuality, and culture, to name a few.

- **Purpose-driven**: OpenHR can be a pillar within your ESG and Social Development strategy. Accessing a blended workforce will help you attract untapped or ignored talent pools globally and locally, providing wider opportunities for an increased workforce mix to get interested in your company, how you do things and how they can be a part of it. It also means your company can have global and local footprints, with localised resources to help reduce the carbon footprint associated with travel, productivity loss of travel time, and much more.

- **Scalability**: Allows easy expansion or reduction in response to business needs. For example, contingent workers can be brought in to handle short-term projects, spikes in demand, or specialised tasks. This could be seen as long-term or a response to short-term needs. It allows a company to scale up or down more easily without the long-term commitment associated with permanent hires.

- **Access to Specialised Skills**: By hiring contingent workers for specialised tasks, companies can tap into expertise that may not be needed full-time but is crucial for certain projects. This keeps the workforce lean and focused while allowing access to the right skills when needed.

- **Innovation**: A blend of different backgrounds can foster creativity and innovation at all levels. This is part of a super-empowered blended workforce supported by growth-centred line managers.

- **Cost Savings**: Organisations like Eventurous, Monzo, and others have all proven that a blended workforce, mixing permanent and independent contractors and workers, is more economical than maintaining a full-time in-house team and the bricks-and-mortar infrastructure that is also required.

- **Risk Mitigation**: If the market conditions change suddenly, having a blended workforce, underpinned by an OpenHR framework, allows companies to adapt more easily without the significant financial impact that laying off permanent staff would entail.

- **Talent Attraction**: Offering contingent roles might attract professionals who prefer the flexibility and variety of temporary assignments or specialised longer-term roles. These could be highly skilled individuals who might otherwise not be interested in full-time positions.

- **Long-Term Open Talent Management:** Utilising contingent workers alongside permanent workers as your formalised blended workforce can also be a way to mix and enhance the skill sets across all employees to fit short-term and longer-term gaps or new, fast-action opportunities that require specialism and high levels of flexibility, globally or locally.

- **Global Reach:** Blending permanent and contingent workers allows businesses to access global talent pools. This supports and enhances remote collaboration and can be particularly beneficial in accessing skills that may be scarce in the local job market.

- **Responsiveness to Market Trends**: A more adaptable workforce allows organisations to respond quickly to market trends and shifts. This agility helps companies stay competitive in a constantly evolving landscape.

- **Employee Development**: Permanent employees can benefit from the varied expertise and fresh perspectives of contingent workers. This can lead to permanent staff professional growth and development opportunities as well as formalised learning opportunities for contingent workers.

- **Work-Life Balance:** The flexibility associated with a blended workforce may also contribute to better work-life balance for both permanent and contingent workers. Each job role can better suit each individual based on their work preferences and needs. This can lead to increased job satisfaction and productivity.

In August 2022, the article in Forbes Magazine *'More Big Companies Are Hiring Freelancers. That's Good News For The Self-Employed,'* by Elaine Pofeldt, highlighted new research from MBO Partners that argues small, medium and large organisations are increasingly buying into the cost/benefit equation of a blended workforce model[74]:

"The average enterprise company reported that 'contingent' labour now makes up 28% of its workforce... The survey found that the top reasons for turning to contingent labour are meeting temporary workload needs, increasing productivity, getting tasks done more quickly and getting access to specialized skills and hard-to-hire talent."

By adopting a systematic approach to managing and accessing a blended workforce underpinned by an OpenHR framework,

---

74   https://www.forbes.com/sites/elainepofeldt/2022/08/30/more-big-companies-are-hiring-freelancers-thats-good-news-for-the-self-employed/

organisations can craft a dynamic, effective, and resourceful work-force tailored to their needs. Acknowledging the inherent benefits and implementing the outlined methods will enable the optimal utilisation of independent workers and, much as, permanent employees.

This comprehensive strategy can enrich the company's competencies, promote innovation, and drive success and growth, positioning the organisation for a future that can adapt to ever-changing market demands.

MEASURING STRATEGIC AND OPERATIONAL PROGRESS

To achieve what we set out above, measuring the effectiveness of your OpenHR framework and formalised blended workforce involves assessing organisational, team, and individual performance—aligned to company goals and the evolution of 'good culture'—regardless of employee designation, location, ways of working, and level.

Here are some suggestions for starting right and building measurables from week 1: First things first - We should clearly define expectations and goals.

Begin by defining what you want to achieve with the blended workforce. Set clear, measurable objectives and communicate these to the blended workers, line management and leaders.

Based on our OpenHR work completed with our clients, here are the most important **strategic key performance indicators (KPIs)** to consider for your own organisation's situation:

- **Outcome-Based Work:** Specify the critical success criteria for your entire workforce for each objective, task, or project, including the line manager's support expectations and deliverables.

- **Quality of Work**: Specify and evaluate the quality of deliverables, ensuring they meet standards and requirements for permanent workers, independent workers, and blended work teams.

- **Timeliness**: Monitor how promptly all workers meet deadlines and create data-based comparisons to identify where OpenHR is working best and where to tighten up:

  - Independent workers only
  - Permanent workers only
  - Where a project, task, objective or drive is being led and managed by a blended workforce.
  - Line Management

- **Communication**: Assess how effectively the blended workforce, managers, and leaders communicate. What works? What needs to be improved? What best practices are emerging to fast-track wider adoption?

- **Adaptability**: Measure how well your blended workforce, managers and leaders adapt to changes or feedback.

- **Cost-Effectiveness**: Evaluate the value provided about the cost and relative benefit. For example, there are the upsides or downsides of using a blended workforce versus permanent workers in terms of cost and added benefits to the business, its customers, and other stakeholders.

To keep on top of progress measurement, week on week, month on month, there are several associated operational implementation actions, considerations, and must-dos to have in place. Treat this list as a menu of options to suit your situation, and cross-check with your approach.

This list represents the OpenHR Dozen. Twelve measures of operational effectiveness of your OpenHR approach and blended workforce success, which both feed directly into the above strategic KPI considerations:

- **Calculate ROI:** Measure the financial impact of your blended workforce on the organisation by establishing clear outcomes, including quantitative (e.g., revenue, costs, productivity, and profit) and qualitative measures (e.g., culture evolution, living our values, changes in behaviour).

- **Evaluate Impact on Business Goals**: Determine the contribution of the blended workforce to overall objectives compared to previous work models.

- **Review and Update Metrics**: Regularly revise KPIs and metrics to align with business priorities, how your blended workforce matures, and how your OpenHR framework works.

- **Management and Peer Review**: Solicit progress assessments from blended workers and line management. This can be achieved through peer-blended worker groups - with and without management representation, and through line manager observation and data.

- **Customer Feedback:** Collect customer feedback around your blended workforce's effectiveness, efficiency, and empathy. For example, what works? What doesn't work? How has the new OpenHR and blended workforce formalisation been a benefit, or otherwise, to the customer? What new practices can be shared across all customer-facing teams to enhance the customer experience delivery? And so on.

- **Regular Check-ins**: Schedule ongoing informal check-ins to discuss progress. Provide feedback and serve as a forum for spotlighting management coaching opportunities and peer support sharing. This includes creating a psychologically safe environment for blended workers to voice concerns and feedback.

- **Leverage Technology:** Use task, productivity, communication, and project management tools to streamline both formal and informal collaboration, regardless of job role or level.

- **Assess Cultural Fit and Engagement**: Evaluate how well your blended workforce integrates and how it builds an evolved company culture and values.

- **Ensure Legal Compliance:** Maintain compliance with relevant laws and regulations when working with independent contractors and gig workers.

- **Understand and execute your attraction and recruitment strategy**: How are you challenging your recruitment agents to change their approach in aid of your more open, blended workforce approach? You will need to understand other routes to recruitment: The right forum (i.e. social networks), platform (i.e. UpWork), policies (i.e. based on country of worker residence; regulations, etc), Remuneration and recognition (i.e. the 'Thrills' room in your OpenHouse)

- **Analyse Retention and Turnover:** Investigate the retention and turnover rates for insights into satisfaction within the blended workforce and how this impacts employee engagement, retention, and attraction.

- **Conduct Entry and Exit Interviews:** Collect insights from arriving and departing workers, both permanent employees and non-employees, to enhance your OpenHR framework, manage and measure it, and improve your blended workforce collaboration and contribution to growth.

HOW WE CAN HELP YOU

To get you started, we both have been involved in multiple OpenHR transformations especially since we came out of the COVID-19 Pandemic of the early 2020s.

We bring this experience to all projects and have case studies, assessments, templates, tools, examples and more, including global expert contacts and like-minded human capital and HR professionals to put you in touch with from a 'sharing best practices' perspective.

In addition, we have worked with large, medium, small and scale-up businesses around the world, as well as working closely with the independent workforce community, including those platforms and companies dedicated, like us, to formalise the blended workforce as the norm.

We see both sides, and we see what works and what doesn't.

OpenHR will undoubtedly look different across organisations. There are large corporations, multinationals, the public sector, government level, and so on. Emphasis may be needed in certain rooms, or a complete makeover of the house may be required. As such, there are various stages of readiness for OpenHR and maturity across organisations to pull it off. Therefore, some organisations may need more of our help than others - even if that is just to get started.

With this in mind, we have a menu of services that may be of assistance to you and your business at each stage of the process. Whether it is to start the conversation, seek buy-in from leadership, create the strategic plan, develop the implementation roadmap, execute the plan, etc.

Below is a table to help you identify exactly where your need is, the outcome you are aiming for, and how we can help you achieve your goals beyond providing you with the book alone. This is to be viewed as a menu of options, not necessarily a step-by-step roadmap.

In the meantime, you can connect and start a conversation with either of us through LinkedIn or through email below:

- **Jeremy Blain:** info@performanceworks.global
- **Dr Rochelle Haynes:** contact@crowdpotential.co.uk

OUR SERVICES FOR YOUR NEEDS AND SITUATION

Pick the most suited option for you or mix and match.

Your need	How we can help	Outcomes
Awareness needs to be raised at all levels of the business. • As a conversation starter internally to build the case for change. • Also applicable to internal conferences, industry events and other business forums	**Keynote and/or leadership briefing** • Detailing the why, what and how-to, backed by relevant data and tailored to your business, industry, and need. • Complete with relevant case studies that consider all perspectives	• An understanding of what is coming, why it is important and what needs to happen next. • An executive leadership buy-in lever

Developing **your strategy** and presentable, compelling story	• **Consulting, facilitation of strategy sessions and group coaching** • This will help you work through and work up the strategy, how it would be presented, and the most appropriate story to tell.	• A robust OpenHR strategy and roadmap, ready to present to the executive leadership and other stakeholders.
Develop your **implementation plan**, including comms planning and an internal engagement strategy with customers.	• **Consulting, facilitation, and coaching support** • To help you work through each component part (often with the inclusion of employee champions and even a customer voice where appropriate)	• A clear blueprint underpinned by robust 90-, 180- and 360-day implementation plans, in parallel with how it will be communicated, executed, measured, and adapted once started (as required) • Buy-in from the organisation and blended workforce to the plan and their role to make it a success

Creating your Rules, Tools, Skills, and Thrills blueprint • One detailed approach, tailored to your organisational needs, for each room within the OpenHouse	**Consulting and/or coaching support** • N.B. This process may take weeks or months, depending on the stage of OpenHR development you and your organisation.	• A deep dive into each OpenHR room and each component part within each room • A clarity of need and action plan for each element across the 4 OpenHouse rooms • Which can feed into the ongoing executive leadership discussions and sponsorship
Creating a solid foundation to support transformation and a 'leak-proof OpenProtect roof' To provide a safe environment for everyone to contribute, experiment and build new ways of working, collaborating, and communicating.	**Consulting, team building, engagement strategies** Small groups / companywide / independents **Culture transformation consulting and action** Access to blueprints and experts from non-competitive organisations and human capital professionals	• To help you demonstrate to the organisation, to customers and employees, that you are 'Doing the right things, in the right way.' • Underpin transformation with a solid evolution of culture to model 'how we do things around here' in values and behaviour terms.

Skills and behaviour building	Consulting/assessment/knowledge and skills building	
Developing the capabilities that enable a blended workforce to thrive, regardless of employee designation, location, culture and more.	(Including pre-activity training/ development needs). • Masterclasses (leaders and senior management) and core-skills training to enable OpenHR. • To support your blended workforce and sponsoring/ supporting management in the optimal core skills to fuel great collaboration, communication, digital working practices and much more.	• A skills matrix for your organisation to suit the blended workforce and newly implemented OpenHR structure. • Appropriate training for all employees, whether permanent or independent contractors, should be provided, and the power of this more flexible, global workforce should be recognised.

Check-ins and best practices feed.	Our OpenHR Best Practices Club	
Ongoing communication is done as regular scheduled events, or as ad hoc requirements for external input and insight.	• Sign up for a monthly virtual exchange session or face-to-face roundtable. (Whatever is appropriate) • Access to both Rochelle and Jeremy to global and local experts, to other human capital professionals to representatives of other, non-competitive, blended workforces and more	• Real-time access to Rochelle and Jeremy • Real-time network of fellow professionals going through similar OpenHR transformations and implementations. • Flexible for you - access based on need, ad hoc or sign up to a series of monthly sharing session

OPENHR GLOSSARY OF GLOSSARIES

The following glossary is intended to aggregate the most common industry terms being used for all aspects of the blended workforce and the modern workplace, to identify the definitive Open Talent and OpenHR lexicons in use.

As we have interrogated sources from all around the world, we have used the source English spelling (i.e. US English where used).

This is split into 5 separate categories, which are:

1. Business terms and expressions

2. Types and ways of working

3. Terms for the workforce and different designations of workers

4. Platform terms

5. Types of associated businesses

For many terms there are multiple ways of explaining them. Therefore, where multiple interpretations are valid, we list them. Otherwise, we have selected the single best fit based on the common terminology being established.

BUSINESS TERMS AND EXPRESSIONS

Term	Definition
Digital Transformation	Digital transformation is the process by which companies embed technologies across their businesses to drive fundamental change. –Accenture, 2023 Digital transformation can refer to anything from IT modernization (for example, cloud computing), to digital optimization, to the invention of new digital business models. The term is widely used in public-sector organizations to refer to modest initiatives such as putting services online or legacy modernization. Thus, the term is more like "digitization" than "digital business transformation." –Gartner, 2023 Digital transformation takes a customer-driven, digital-first approach to all aspects of a business, from its business models to customer experiences to processes and operations. –IBM, 2023

Employment

Employment is defined as persons of working age who were engaged in any activity to produce goods or provide services for pay or profit, whether at work during the reference period or not at work due to temporary absence from a job, or to working-time arrangement.

–World Bank

Any activity performed by persons of any sex and age to produce goods or to provide services for use by others or for own use.

–ILO, 2019

E-Recruitment

Refers to methods and processes undertaken by sourcers and recruiters which rely significantly on electronic platforms like job boards, social networks and other online labor platforms, to find candidates. This is different from "online staffing" in which no sourcers or recruiters are involved.

–SIA Lexicon

Future of Work

The future of work describes changes in how work will get done over the next decade, influenced by technological, generational and social shifts.

–JWH, 2023

Gig Economy

The Gig economy refers to various forms of temporary jobs whereby organisations and independent workers engage in short-term work arrangements in a free market system. The definition covers freelancers, consultants, independent contractors and professionals. Some work through online platforms, while others connect with partners and contacts off-platform.

-Freetrade Europa, 2023

The gig economy uses digital platforms to connect freelancers with customers to provide short-term services or asset-sharing.

-World Economic Forum, 2021

Industry 4.0

The Fourth Industrial Revolution, 4IR, or Industry 4.0 conceptualizes rapid change to technology, industries, and societal patterns and processes in the 21st century due to increasing interconnectivity and smart automation. Coined popularly by the World Economic Forum Founder and Executive Chairman, Klaus Schwab, it asserts that the changes seen are more than just improvements to efficiency but express a significant shift in industrial capitalism.

-Wikipedia, 2021

It is characterized by a fusion of technologies that is blurring the lines between the physical, digital, and biological spheres.

-World Economic Forum, 2016

Industry 4.0, cont'd

The fourth industrial revolution will take what was started in the third with the adoption of computers and automation and enhance it with smart and autonomous systems fuelled by data and machine learning.

-Bernard Marr (Forbes, 2018)

Industry 4.0—also called the Fourth Industrial Revolution or 4IR—is the next phase in the digitization of the manufacturing sector, driven by disruptive trends including the rise of data and connectivity, analytics, human-machine interaction, and improvements in robotics.

-McKinsey, 2022

Industry 4.0 refers to the "smart" and connected production systems that are designed to sense, predict, and interact with the physical world, so as to make decisions that support production in real-time. In manufacturing, it can increase productivity, energy efficiency, and sustainability. It increases productivity by reducing downtime and maintenance costs.

-UNCTAD, 2022

On-Demand Economy

Economic activity generated by technology (ex. an internet platform or app) that immediately fulfils a consumer demand. In this case, a transaction of work - of a fixed duration - facilitated by technology and involves hiring one or more contingent workers.

-Open Assembly, 2023

Open Innovation

A strategy that suggests the best ideas, solutions, and people necessary to solve your organisation's difficult problems may come from outside your company entirely. There are different types of open innovation – contests, crowdsourcing, collaborative communities and online labour markets – and the term includes the way to adopt and implement open innovation in an organisation.

-Harvard Business School, 2023

Innovation that happens through the interactions of internal and external ideas, technologies, processes and channels. As opposed to closed innovation, where innovation typically happens within company boundaries, or within a self-contained environment with rigid structures.

-Open Assembly, 2018

Open Talent Strategy

How companies leverage communities or pools of non-full-time employees to achieve critical business outcomes.

-Open Assembly, 2018

Open Talent Economy

A collaborative, technology-driven, rapid-cycle way of doing business.

-Deloitte, 2013

A large ecosystem of "open-sourced" talent where people can connect, share information and build community.

-Open Assembly, 2018

Payroll

Payroll for freelancers typically refers to the process of calculating and distributing payments to independent contractors, who are not considered employees of a company. Freelancers typically invoice their clients for services rendered and are responsible for tracking their own work hours and expenses. Overall, while the process of payroll for freelancers differs from that of traditional employees, it is still an important aspect of financial management for businesses that work with independent contractors.

-Freelance Business Community, 2023

Platform Economy

A form of organizing paid work through digital platforms.

-Freetrade Europa, 2023

Project Economy

The Project Economy is where individuals focus on their skills, talents and capabilities, in order to carry out time-specific paid tasks, often for multiple employers. What is more, a key driver is flexibility and the desire to adjust "working life" to fit in with "private life" - and not the other way around.

-Freetrade Europa, 2023

Self-Employment/ Self-Employed

If a person is a business owner or contractor that provides services to other businesses, either directly or through a personal services company (PSC),1 they will generally be considered to be self-employed.

-CIPD, 2021

A person who is the sole or joint owner of the unincorporated enterprise (one that has not been incorporated, i.e. formed into a legal corporation) in which they work, unless they are also in paid employment which is their main activity.

-European Commission,

This term refers to companies who allow workers to be self-employed (egenanställda) - a status which does not exist in countries such as Sweden. Self-employment companies allow individuals to send invoices and be paid for work without the need to have a company. The self-employment company takes care of paying taxes and social security as well as compliance and general responsibility for health and safety.

-Freetrade Europa, 2023

An individual who operates a business or profession as a sole proprietor, independent contractor or consultant.

-Open Assembly, 2018

Sharing Economy

The Sharing Economy can be characterised as only relating to activities that involve peer to peer transactions. This can, therefore, be defined as an economic system where assets or services are shared between private individuals, for compensation, facilitated using the internet (e.g. renting out property).

-Freetrade Europa, 2023

Statement of Work (SOW)

A legally binding contract between a client and a vendor, supplier or worker that captures and defines all the work management or work requirement aspects of a project.

-Open Assembly, 2023

Talent Acquisition

The ongoing process of attracting, sourcing, recruiting, and hiring talent (all worker types) for an organization.

-Open Assembly, 2023 (Adapted from SIA Lexicon)

VUCA/ VUCAD   A checklist against which businesses can map the relative disruptions to their way of working. The acronym stands for Volatile, Uncertain, Complex and Ambiguous and the D stands for Distributed to recognise the increasingly dispersed nature of our workforces.

-Open Assembly, 2018

An acronym representing the characteristics of the key disruptions to traditional approaches to working. Volatile, Uncertain, Complex, Ambiguous, Distributed.

-Haynes and Blain, 2020

TYPES OF WORKING

Agency Work   Agency work is an internationally recognised and regulated form of employment. The agency worker has an employment contract with the employment agency. They are then deployed to a user firm and work under the guidance and supervision of the user company.

-World Employment Confederation, 2023

Collective   A way for freelancers to work as a team without the constraints of a company structure. In comparison to solo freelancing, these teams can tackle larger contracts (with bigger payoffs) and better leverage individual skills.

-Robin Moreau, Medium.com (2020)

Co-creation Adding new value based on collaboration from more than one source or expert. For example, ideas, products or solutions that are generated from crowdsourcing and/or the coming together of key stakeholders and consumers.

-Open Assembly, 2021

Contest A competition, managed via a talent platform on behalf of an enterprise client, in which participants are invited to solve a challenge. Winners receive a monetary prize.

-Open Assembly, 2021

Contract Services Well-defined services delivered by an individual or organization as laid out in a contract.

SIA Lexicon

Co-working An office where several people can work independently in the same space, get to know each other at work and exchange experiences. It's similar to a regular office environment, but here the coworkers are not colleagues but independent professionals or employees of a company who can work from anywhere. In the co-working offices, anyone can rent a workstation that is available for an hourly rate or with a daily or monthly pass.

-Freelance Business Community, 2023

Co-Working Spaces

A workplace environment in which people, who are usually from different companies, share office space and work collaboratively. Most spaces provide open plan workspace along with private offices, meeting rooms, lounge areas, and other shared amenities such as printers, copiers and kitchen space.

-Allwork, 2019

Crowdsourcing

Information, talent, ideas, content or something else accessed by a large number of people, paid or unpaid, often using a platform (ex. Waze).

-Open Assembly, 2019

Elastic Teams

This refers to the provision of skilled individuals and teams on-demand, via platforms. This allows companies to scale-up and down services such as marketing, sales, operations, software development and testing. This on-demand approach is rising in response to the lack of full-time skilled talent in a number of fields.

-Freetrade Europa, 2023

Fractional Work/ Worker/ Hire

Fractional hire combines consulting and freelancing, and usually for senior positions and long-term assignments. Freelancers can be hired for a fractional role. Or this position can be open for a fixed part-time hire.

-Freelance Business Community, 2023

Freelancing

The way you work as a freelancer.

-Freelance Business Community, 2023

Full-time Work/ 9 to 5 Job This refers to a work arrangement where employees turn up at a workplace and work set hours. These jobs mostly involve working five days a week in an office setting. The individual employed has a permanent employment contract, and a set salary as well as receives benefits including holiday pay, sick leave and a pension. In some quarters, the term is used pejoratively to describe uninspiring and dull traditional corporate set ups.

-Freetrade Europa, 2023

Gig-Style Working A way of providing value to a company or more than one company, using unique skill sets and expertise, which falls outside traditional employment classifications.

-Open Assembly, 2019

Hybrid Work This refers to a flexible work model that supports a blend of in-office, remote, and on-the-go workers. It offers employees the autonomy to choose to work wherever and however they are most productive. In some arrangements workers will be required to come to the office (normally 2-3 days a week).

-Freetrade Europa, 2023

Hybrid is used to describe something of mixed character; composed of mixed parts. In the context of Open Talent, Hybrid is often used to describe the workplace and the workforce. A hybrid workplace describes a scenario that involves combining time working from home and time in physical proximity to colleagues at a workplace. A Hybrid workforce describes a combination of internally controlled workers and external workers.

-Open Assembly, 2023

Hybrid Program A contingent workforce program management strategy that involves blending different sourcing model attributes. Typically, a hybrid program would include elements of vendor-neutral as well as master-supplier programs. For example, a buyer might engage a single provider to act as the sole supplier for its *Light Industrial* job requisitions while having multiple providers competitively bid on IT positions.

-SIA Lexicon, 2021

Outsourcing

Outsourcing refers to a contractual arrangement wherein a company hires another company or an individual to take charge of a particular activity that is currently or could be performed in-house.

-Freelance Business Community, 2023

Remote Work

Remote work is a type of flexible working arrangement that allows an employee to work from remote locations outside of corporate offices.

-Freetrade Europa, 2023

Work that is performed outside of a traditional office environment, by an employee who sits from a local coworking space, from home, in a city or somewhere else.

-Open Assembly, 2018

Self-employed

This is the practice of working for oneself to earn money, rather than an employer. In many countries, this entails a separate, specific tax regime too. Furthermore, self-employed workers can access an additional layer of service providers who support self-employed workers with administrative and support services.

-Freetrade Europa, 2023

**Side-Gig/
Side Hustle**

A job that gives the employee extra income while working full-time.

-Freelance Business Community, 2023

A side hustle is an umbrella term for all types of employment undertaken in addition to one's full-time job. A side hustle is generally freelance or project work which provides supplemental income. Side hustles are often - but not exclusively - things a person is passionate about, rather than a typical 9 to 5 day job which is taken to purely earn money and make ends meet.

-Freetrade Europa, 2023

**Strategic
Workforce
Planning**

The process an organization undertakes to develop a holistic, long-term and proactive approach to strategically assessing and accessing all multiple forms of talent engagement. Specifically, Strategic Workforce Planning links corporate and strategic objectives and their associated workforce implications with multiple avenues of talent engagement and resourcing (Direct Hire, Contingent, SOW, Outsource, etc.).

-SIA Lexicon

Synchronous vs. asynchronous Terminology that came to prominence in the world of programming and has found resonance in the world of task management, learning and organizational development. Synchronous work is done by groups of people working at the same time. Asynchronous work can be done by people working to their own schedules and at their own pace and is conducive to remote work.

-Open Assembly, (CTO), 2023

Telecommuting Working at home, or at another off-site location, for an organization whose office is located elsewhere, with two-way communication via technology.

-SIA Lexicon, 2021

TERMS FOR WORKFORCE/WORKERS

Agency Worker

This refers to a temporary employee, typically an office worker, who finds employment through a temporary staffing agency. Agency workers are usually brought in when another person is absent or when there is a period of extra work. In the US, the term "staffing" is used.

-Freetrade Europa, 2023

If you're an agency worker, your contract is with the employment agency. They place you with a company ('hiring organisation') for a temporary period of work ('assignment'). When you're on an assignment, the hiring organisation is responsible for directing your work.

-ACAS, 2023

Blended Workforce

A mix of permanent workforce (employees), flexible workforce (freelancers) and technology (software), with the aim of finding out how they can work together to form a powerful team.

-Freelance Business Community, 2023

The mix of permanent and independent workers who work together to fulfil a project or professional need. Can also refer to diversity within the workforce in terms of generation, online/offline, etc. Also referred to as the Mixed Workforce.

-The Blended Workforce Revolution (Crowd Potential, 2020)

A workforce made up of a combination of permanent employees and freelancers on flexible contracts.

-Freetrade Europa, 2023

Blended workforce means the planned use of direct-hire personnel and contingent workers to meet the strategic and tactical workforce needs of a corporation.

-SIA Lexicon

Certified Contingent Workforce Professional (CCWP)

An accreditation program provided by Staffing Industry Analysts designed for HR, procurement, MSP solution providers and others who manage corporate contingent staffing. The CCWP Certification assesses and expands the level of expertise of participants to create an elite brand of CW program management professionals. To become certified, participants must demonstrate knowledge of contingent workforce management best practices by taking a class and passing a rigorous certification exam.

-SIA Lexicon, 2021

Consultant

A consultant is a professional who provides advice and other purposeful activities in an area of specialisation. Consultants can work for companies or individuals, as an independent professional or owners of a company, or as an employee of a local or international consultancy firm.

-Freelance Business Community, 2023

This is a person who provides expert advice to companies and organisations for a fee. This type of professional is an expert in a specific field and can work for a consultancy firm or be an independent contractor. In Europe, a consultant is often classed as being highly skilled and someone who carries out complex and well-paid assignments.

-Freetrade Europa, 2023

Contingent Worker/Labour on Demand

A professional who works with companies on a project / temporary basis, for a certain fee for their services, sometimes on an hourly basis. A very similar, almost identical term is Contractor, Freelancer, Interim Manager or Independent Professional.

-Freelance Business Community, 2023

A contingent worker is someone who is hired for a fixed period of time, often on a project basis. Examples of contingent workers are freelancers, consultants, part-timers, on-call workers, independent contractors, and people in other types of alternative work arrangements.

-AIHR, 2023

Workers that work only when needed, including contingent workers, SOWs, ICs, and freelancers.

-SIA Lexicon, 2021

Contractor

A professional or company that carries out an assignment under the terms of a contract. This can be intellectual work, but also physical work (e.g. electrical installation). They usually work for one client at a time, full-time or for the length of a project, and typically work at the clients' office.

-Freelance Business Community, 2023

An individual hired to deliver a specified service as laid out in a contract. In some organizations this term is used interchangeably with "temporary employee" to refer to individuals employed by a temporary staffing firm, typically at a professional level.

-SIA Lexicon, 2021

Crowd

A group of people who come together to complete a task, project or outcome, regardless of whether they sit in- or outside the organization. The essence of the "crowd" is one of co-creation, iteration, and collaboration amongst parties incentivized to contribute based on interest and/ or competition.

-Open Assembly, 2019

Digital Nomads   A subset of independent workers. Can be nomadic and 'location-free' but sometimes work from a single remote location. Location-independent workers who are digital natives, use digital tools to complete tasks and rarely, if ever, have face-to-face contact with their clients or employers. Can be on full-time contracts as well as ad hoc.

-Crowd Potential, 2020

This refers to a person who earns a living working online in various locations of their choosing (rather than a fixed business location).

-Freetrade Europa, 2023

Digital nomads are people who are location-independent and use technology to perform their job, living a nomadic lifestyle. Digital nomads work remotely, telecommuting rather than being physically present at a company's headquarters or office.

-Investopedia, 2021

| **Distributed Workforce** | An alternative to a co-located workforce, a distributed workforce is made of workers who are based in multiple locations including offices, satellites, home and other places. COVID-19 induced lockdowns have increased the prevalence of distributed workforces.

-Centre for the Transformation of Work

A distributed workforce is said to exist when a business utilizes employees who work in multiple locations, including their homes and satellite offices.

-VM Ware, 2023 |

Elastic Teams — Full-time or part-time employees on the company payroll. Typically enjoy employment-related benefits such as regular salary, paid leave, sick pay, and collective representation.

-Freelance Business Community, 2023

Flexible Workforce/ On-Demand Workforce — A workforce that works for a company in a flexible way, other than the traditional 9 to 5. From a company's point of view, this is about workers who are available quickly, who can work on temporary assignments and who can adapt flexibly to the tasks that arise.

-Freelance Business Community, 2023

Freelancer

Highly skilled professionals who sell their expertise on a project basis to multiple clients per year in a variety of fields. This typically includes marketing, media, IT and engineering services, graphic design, design, translation, interpreting, business consulting and coaching. They work on a flexible schedule, in a location of their choice, typically online. They usually only need a computer to complete their tasks. A.k.a. contractor or independent professional.

-Freelance Business Community, 2023

This refers to a person who is self-employed and does not necessarily have a long-term contract with one specific employer. Freelancers can be represented by a company or an agency that resells freelance labour to clients, while others work independently or use professional associations, platforms or websites to find work. Freelancing covers all sectors as well as levels of skills and experience.

-Freetrade Europa, 2023

Typically classified as independent contractors, freelancers are independent professional workers who aren't paid as salaried employees and perform, or have the freedom to perform, multiple jobs at one time for multiple clients

-Open Assembly, 2019

Gig Worker

An independent worker who does work for a company's clients. The term is typically used to describe work that technological developments have opened up, such as freelancing on online platforms (Upwork, Fiverr, etc.), or jobs provided by the rise of the sharing economy (Uber, Deliveroo, Etsy, etc.).

-Freelance Business Community, 2023

Someone who works part time, or full time, in the gig economy. In Europe and the US this has been used in the media as an umbrella term for low-skilled, low-paid workers in precarious situations who do not have a traditional job contract.

-Freetrade Europa, 2023

Workers who perform project-based or freelance work. Any contingent or temporary worker, sourced directly, through an online platform, app or agency, which provides work for a finite period of time and managed by a variety of providers. Also called "on-demand" or "human cloud" workers.

-Open Assembly, 2019

Global Workforce Ecosystem

Networks of talent, information and technology that exist both inside and outside companies, used to create a global culture of workers who pursue their passions and work more efficiently.

-Open Assembly, 2019

Independent or Contingent Worker

Self-employed workers, usually professional with some form of expertise. Often work remotely using digital tools to communicate and collaborate. Responsible for billing clients and sourcing work. Also often referred to as the Invisible Workforce or Alternative Workforce.

-Crowd Potential, 2020

Independent Contractor

An independent contractor can be a synonym for a freelancer and is necessarily self-employed. Very often, independent contractors work across a number of clients and even sectors (e.g. IT, professional services and building sectors). Employed staff on full time contracts who are hired out to third-party companies and organisations are agency workers.

-Freetrade Europa, 2023

A self-employed person who is in an independent trade, business or profession in which they offer their services to the general public and has the right to control or direct only the result of the work and not what will be done and how it will be done.

-IRS, 2024

Open Talent

Open Talent is the digital extension of outsourcing. It refers to the 'crowd' of global talent available outside a company's internal hires. Hundreds of companies and platforms comprise this large ecosystem of "open-sourced" talent enabling people and organisations to find the best ideas at scale, tap the best expertise, and augment staffing as needed.

-Open Assembly, 2023

The open talent economy is a social environment where people can connect, share information, and build a sense of community outside of a rigid corporate structure. They can also work on different projects for a number of different companies and organisations. The open talent economy therefore gives employers the power to choose when and who they employ, while workers have the power to choose when they work, where and for whom. Open talent is also characterised by a shift from traditional organisational structures to dynamic networks.

-Freetrade Europa, 2023

Platform Worker

Someone who works part time, or full time, in the platform economy. Platform workers are accessed online to provide a wide variety of paid services.

-Freetrade Europa, 2023

Remote Worker

Someone who works remotely partly or all of the time. Remote workers can be employed or a freelancer/self-employed person.

-Freetrade Europa, 2023

Solopreneur/ Solo Entrepreneur

An individual who starts and runs a business independently and autonomously, without a co-founder or employees.

-Freelance Business Community, 2023

This is someone who works independently and does not hire employees or other team members.

-Freetrade Europa, 2023

PLATFORM TERMS

Contract Management

A software or a process that helps to manage contracts made with customers, vendors, partners, or employees.

-Freelance Business Community, 2023

Digital Sourcing Platform

A platform that helps companies in finding and qualifying freelance or full-time talents using technology to streamline the process. In addition to running the platform, there is a strong emphasis on the active involvement in the selection process.

-Freelance Business Community, 2023

Online Staffing Platforms	A sub-segment of the Human Cloud, an online staffing platform enables specific hirers and specific (typically contingent) workers to enter into, complete and transact work arrangements most often virtually with resources anywhere in the world. It is the oldest Human Cloud model (arising in the early 2000s). There is typically a direct legal relationship between the hirer and worker, which the platform enables. -SIA Lexicon, 2021
Open Talent Platform/ Open Talent Marketplace	An online, often self-service application that matches on-demand talent or gig workers with work that needs to get done inside organizations. -Open Assembly, 2018
Taskify/ Taskification	The process of reducing or fragmenting a "Job" or a "Scope of Work" down to its most "basic tasks" or steps. These granular "tasks" can now be divided and allocated to multiple workers, either within the organization or outside the organization. -Open Assembly, 2023 The auditing jobs and identifying each task to increase productivity and give more assignments to temporary workers. -Adapted from Yale Global

Talent Platform   A talent marketplace is a technology-enabled platform that connects employees with potential positions and developmental opportunities within the organization.

-AIHR, 2022

TYPES OF BUSINESSES

Agency   A business providing a service to another business, person or group.

-Oxford Languages

Decentralized autonomous organization (DAO)   A decentralized autonomous organization is a member-run entity, built on blockchain and smart contracts. It has no centralized management and encourages decision-making by members who vote on proposals. Members join by acquiring cryptocurrency tokens which give them a stake in the DAO.

-Center for the Transformation of Work, 2021

Freelance Management System (FMS)   An online platform that facilitates all operational, financial and legal aspects of clients' cooperation with freelancers, from application to payment.

-Freelance Business Community, 2023

Managed Service Provider (MSP)/Managed Services

A company that takes on primary responsibility for managing an organisation's contingent workforce program. Typical responsibilities of an MSP include overall program management, reporting and tracking, supplier selection and management, order distribution and often consolidated billing. Many MSPs also provide their clients with a Vendor Management System (VMS). An MSP can also be responsible for the client's direct sourcing and may or may not be independent of a staffing supplier.

-Freelance Business Community, 2023

The practice of outsourcing the responsibility for maintaining and anticipating the need for a contingent workforce. In the world of temporary staffing, these arrangements are also known as managed service providers (MSPs).

-SIA Lexicon, 2021

Freelance Platform/ Freelance Marketplace/ Online staffing platform

Online platforms where clients and freelancers find each other for project-based / hourly collaborations. The freelance platforms typically deduct a commission from the service fee paid by the client to the freelancer, from which they ensure the smooth running of the platform (and generate a profit).

A sub-segment of the Human Cloud, an online staffing platform enables specific hirers and specific (typically contingent) workers to enter, complete and transact work arrangements most often virtually with resources anywhere in the world. It is the oldest Human Cloud model (arising in the early 2000s). There is typically a direct legal relationship between the hirer and worker, which the platform enables.

–Business Community, 2023

Human Cloud

An emerging set of work intermediation models that enable work arrangements of various kinds to be established and completed (including payment of workers) entirely through a digital/ online platform.

–SIA Lexicon (Adapted by Open Assembly), 2021

Microbusiness/ Microenterprise

A microenterprise or microbusiness is a company that employs 10 people or less, has less than EUR 50,000 in start-up funding and typically earns a modest yearly revenue (less than EUR 100,000).

Microbusinesses often specialise in selling a product or service, and these can take different commercial forms: sole-proprietorship, partnership or corporation.

-Freetrade Europa, 2023

Vendor Management System (VMS)

Vendor management system is a software that helps organisations to manage their contingent workforce. It includes the management of vendor relationships, the measurement of vendor performance, procurement, management of contingent workers sourced either through a staffing agency or another sourcing avenue.

-Freelance Business Community, 2023

Afterword

The emergence of the blended workforce, consisting of full-time, part-time, and independent or contingent workers, is an unmistakable phenomenon. This is the era of a more open and flexible workforce globally, in which conventional organisational structures, the workforce and the very ways we work are facing unprecedented challenges.

A radical transformation is taking place in the employment landscape. However, this change seems to be a complex maze that business leaders, HR experts, and even independent workers struggle to comprehend – a significant finding that surfaced in our international research.

As we entered 2024, we brought into focus 8 central pillars to ensure the success of your blended workforce and specific OpenHR manifesto for your organisation:

Clear Direction and Executive Leadership Buy-In: Boards and C-Suite leaders need to understand the significance and benefits of an open workforce and the parallel need for an OpenHR framework to manage it effectively. Without it, any strategic and operational execution could fail before it even starts. HR and human capital professionals' first job is to 'sell' the need and the solution to leaders and the rest of the organisation before anything can accelerate.

The Need for a Structured Approach: Corporations are lagging in structuring and managing their independent and permanent workers in the modern era and how they are integrating both into a formalised blended workforce. There is a need for a clear system of responsibility, expectations, and project management.

Variation in Relationships: Independent workers rely on mutual understanding and trust rather than strict terms. Clear rules and frameworks are necessary for successful relationships.

Clash Between Traditional vs. Digital Ways of Working: The gap in digital skills is a barrier for both HR professionals and independent workers. Investing in digital skills development is essential.

Cultural and Mindset Change: The corporate world must change its approach to attracting, retaining, and managing independent workers. Equality in treatment with full-time staff and adequate support and recognition are key.

Shift Towards Long-term Contracts: Long-term or retainer contracts provide security and help build strong, beneficial relationships between independent workers and their clients.

Lack of Understanding of the Blended Workforce: Many at the corporate level are unaware of the shifts and trends impacting their organisations. Education and adaptation to the growing and diversifying workforce are crucial.

Urgent Need for an integrated framework to bring all the above into focus: Business leaders must acknowledge the diversity within the independent workforce and create strategies tailored to various types of workers.

In response, Our OpenHR approach is visualised within an OpenHouse consisting of four principal rooms to help you implement all the necessary systems, processes, digital tools, and human-centred components to make your blended workforce a success. Our four rooms are:

- **Rules** - Structures and frameworks for success

- **Tools** - Binding ecosystem with enabling technology to fuel human connection, collaboration and communication

- **Skills** - The new knowledge, skills and behaviours to supercharge your blended workforce

- **Thrills** - These are the ways to motivate, recognise, and reward your blended workforce, building engagement, motivation, a sense of community, and enjoyment.

The purpose behind this book has been to provide you with the rationale for why this is now an urgent and important step forward for your organisation. We have also defined the blended workforce and the corresponding need for a new human capital management framework, which we call OpenHR.

More importantly, we have provided the blueprint for creating your own OpenHR framework and getting the component parts in place, and the framework executed as part of your successful blended workforce implementation.

Thank you from both of us for reading our book. We look forward to hearing from you as you accelerate progress in your world.

Make OpenHR your future for a successful, integrated, engaged and high-performing blended workforce.

–Jeremy and Rochelle

Meet the Authors

Jeremy Blain
Founder and CEO, Performance Works International

Founder and CEO, <u>Performance Works International</u> (PWI);

Executive Director of the <u>Transformational Leadership Acceleration Institute</u>;

Managing Partner, <u>DiversITy-Talent</u> (A social enterprise)

Connect on LinkedIn: <u>www.linkedin.com/in/jeremyblain/</u>

Jeremy is the multi-award-winning Chief Executive of Performance Works International (PWI), a modern leadership research and learning journeys company that helps organisations, executive boards, leaders, and teams succeed in the digital climate amidst disruption, opportunity, and uncertainty.

Jeremy has been recognized recently for this by The Independent newspaper, UK, and business, their reporter magazine, as the winner of the 'Best of Global Business 2023' Award for his work in leadership, workforce, and business transformation.

Jeremy combines business and digital transformation expertise, leadership knowledge and commercial success as an international CEO and executive board officer in the UK and Asia, with his experience as a corporate learning and human capital professional of over 25 years.

Jeremy now helps boards, leaders, and managers define strategies to implement digital and human transformations in the modern workplace, with buy-in, involvement, and a foundation of psychological safety across the business through a robust learning and development path.

In parallel, Jeremy has produced and hosted his own multi-platform 'Rethink Leadership' Podcast since 2020, which is now one of the top 1.5% of podcasts globally, also available to watch on YouTube, bringing new leadership and transformation next practices from global experts to an international audience.

He is also one of the foremost global experts on empowered distributed leadership, backed up by his international #1 best-selling book: *Unleash the Inner CEO – Make Distributed Leadership a Reality*. At the time of publishing *Unleash the Inner CEO* has been named the best business leadership book of 2024, picking up the Gold Medal at The Global Book Awards in August 2024.

Jeremy is a regular Keynote speaker, researcher, and author of over 30 industry white papers. He is also a media commentator and has received coverage in high-profile publications, including Forbes, CEO Today, Medium, The Times of London, Dialogue by DUKE CE, Business Matters, HRM, HR Online, and more.

Dr. Rochelle Haynes
BA, MA, PhD, CIPD, HEA

Rochelle is a published author, global speaker, HR consultant, senior lecturer, and the Founder and CEO of <u>Crowd Potential Consulting Inc</u>. She holds a Master's (with Distinction) in Human Resource Management and a PhD in International Human Resource Management. Rochelle's passion lies in applying good people management practices within the growing digital economy, and she has travelled across the globe, including Indonesia and Thailand, to explore the world's top remote-working hotspots and co-working spaces and interview globally dispersed talent. She specialises in OpenHR™, a term she coined to describe the discipline of using HRM to help companies enhance their working relationships with contract or 'open talent,' including digital nomads and other offsite stakeholders whose physical contact with organisations is limited or non-existent.

Rochelle has lectured in several UK universities, including most recently, the University of the West of England (UWE Bristol), where she led Performance Management and Global People Management modules. She recently accepted a post as Senior Lecturer in the Department of Human Resource Management at Nottingham Trent University, an award-winning, business-driven, and globally recognised institution. In the UK, she was nationally commended for her role with the Chartered Institute of Personnel Development (CIPD) as an employability mentor. She has worked all over the world and given global keynotes for many reputable companies, including The Financial Times, BambooHR, Chartered Institute of Personnel Development (CIPD), The Central Bank of Barbados, Hays Marketing Group, and Banco Santander.

Rochelle has been featured in several well-recognised publications, including Forbes, HR Online, and Personnel Today, and she is also a regular guest on several podcasts. In 2020 she started her own podcast called Remotely Speaking Up, where she interviews industry experts on topics related to the future of work. Rochelle is also a member of **Open Assembly, Center for the Transformation of Work,** and ***Keynote***, a global directory of female thought leaders. She also spoke at BambooHR 2022 global conference (headlined by Serena Williams and Simon Sinek).

She also spoke at BambooHR 2022 global conference (headlined by Serena Williams and Simon Sinek). A few of her most recent appointments include a non-executive board member at the London Churchill College, the Head of Research for the Association for the Future of Work, and Future of Work Advisor with Future Catapult within the Barbados Prime Minister's Office.

Acknowledgements

A message from Jeremy Blain:

The first person I would like to recognise is my co-author, Dr. Rochelle Haynes. It has been an absolute blast discussing, researching, testing, and ultimately publishing something that has not been done before in a legacy discipline like human resources. It's been a great ride, Rochelle. Thanks for your amazing insights, good humour, expertise, and friendship. We did it!

I thank all those leaders, human resources and human capital professionals who helped us with this book. As a sounding board, as an interviewee and occasionally a sympathetic ear as we got into the details.

Creating a new framework for anything is difficult, especially for human capital management. That said, Rochelle and I have been determined to put a stake in the ground and build an OpenHR approach globally as an iterative framework and way of managing, measuring, and rewarding our most precious asset, our people, whatever their employment designation.

We have been blessed with a network of interviewees across both human resources and the independent workforce. I want to thank each and every one of them for their time and agreement to be part of this journey, making the concepts in this book come alive and show very clearly the 'how to'. Which is, of course, the be-all and end-all.

A huge thanks and big love to my family, who exclaimed, 'Not another one!' when I announced this project! You have all supported me every step, and I couldn't be more grateful to you.

A message from Dr. Rochelle Haynes:

I've got to thank Jeremy first as God knows we're as opposite as humanly possible when it comes to writing and work styles. Thank you for inspiring me, keeping us on track, and pushing me along the way when needed. You've been an excellent mentor throughout the years, and I continue to enjoy learning from you and working with you. It's great to finally make this dream into reality and bring together seven years of research and work adventures.

I would be nowhere without the love of my God, my friends and my family. Thank you for helping to hold a mirror up to myself on occasion. Thank you for telling me I can do all things when I thought I couldn't. Thank you for always being honest with me about when I needed to pull back or when I needed to give more.

Thank you to my father (recently deceased) who gifted me with his entrepreneurial spirit and outside-the-box thinking. You taught me from young that it doesn't matter where you've started but where you're going and who's journeying with you, and I've been truly blessed with the best travel companions.

To my best friends, Chris Lee, Deviraj Gill and Monique Mayers, thank you for being there through the different chapters of this journey called life. Your encouragement and support during the most challenging of times as well as the best of times has been unwavering. Our lives have truly evolved from school and university days and it's amazing to have people to see and appreciate every version of me. I love you to the moon and back.

Made in the USA
Monee, IL
07 July 2026

56551153R00164